Lands of
THE SETTING SUN

Lands of
THE SETTING SUN

DISCOVERING ALASKA AND WESTERN CANADA

by Bob Devine

NATIONAL GEOGRAPHIC
WASHINGTON, D.C.

CONTENTS

Introduction 6

Traveling THE MARINE HIGHWAY 10
Majesty in detail 40

No road to THESE GRAND LANDS 46
Where the wild things are 68

Across the waters of KACHEMAK BAY 74
Wilderness outposts 104

Deep into ALASKA'S INTERIOR 110
Putting nature's pieces together 130

Nature that GOES ON FOREVER 136
Getting there 156

Highway to the FAR NORTH AND FARTHER 162
The Far North 180

Information for Travelers 186
Acknowledgments 188
Index 189

In Kachemak Bay on the Kenai Peninsula, Gull Island (pages 2-3) provides a nesting site not just for gulls but for thousands of seabirds. A snow-dusted conifer (left) in Tombstone Territorial Park along the Yukon's Dempster Highway hints at how winter is never far away.

A lone campfire illuminates the late-night sky along the Yukon River in Canada.

Introduction

W HEN I GOT THE ASSIGNMENT TO WRITE THIS BOOK, I PULLED the globe down from my bookshelf to my desk. I had to crane my neck to see southeast Alaska—the southernmost region I'd be covering. I actually had to stand up and look down on the top of the globe to see the Arctic Coast of northwest Canada, where my journey would end.

At that point it dawned on me that I was not merely going north from my home in Oregon; I was going to the Far North, a land of myth and mystery to most of us, a place that looms large in our imaginations. It's the legendary realm of hulking grizzlies, glaciers that calve icebergs into the sea, boldly colored totem poles, absurdly cute sea otters, thickly forested islands, independent-minded backwoodsmen, 60-pound salmon, yellow-eyed wolves, the continent's highest mountain, mile-wide braided rivers, and waves of treeless tundra.

Yet these are not the stuff of legends. I know, because I saw them all. It took a bit of effort— hiking, rafting, kayaking, backroads driving, venturing out in small planes and small boats. I soldiered on during lousy weather, but I didn't have to climb mountains or backpack a hundred miles. The Far North has so little civilization that the wilds come right up to the road or the back door.

I started in Ketchikan, a town that would seem extremely remote and rural in the lower 48. But here, it's the equivalent of Chicago. Only two other towns I visited compared in size. I actually drove through a town with a population of one. The number was posted on an official government sign.

As I increased my distance from the Equator, I thought back to the globe in my office. I recalled how empty these regions had appeared. But now I know that the supposed emptiness was simply the result of the globemakers' human-centric perspective. From nature's point of view, the lands through which I passed brimmed with wonders too numerous to show on any globe or map. ■

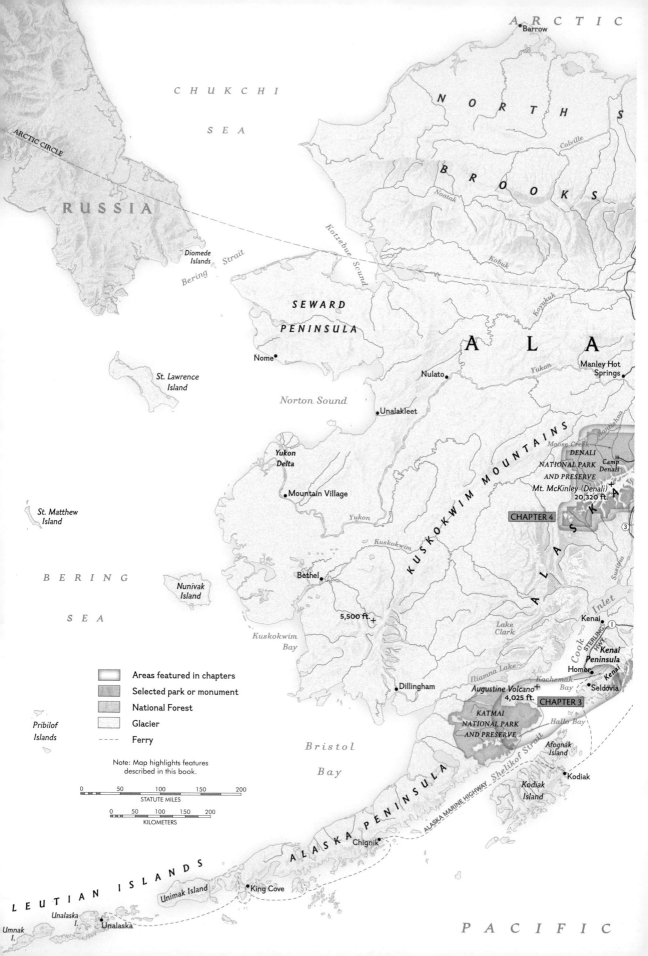

A R C T I C

Barrow

C H U K C H I

S E A

N O R T H S

RUSSIA

ARCTIC CIRCLE

Diomede
Islands

Bering   *Strait*

B R O O K S

Colville

Noatak

Kotzebue Sound

Kobuk

Koyukuk

S E W A R D
P E N I N S U L A

A L A

Nome

St. Lawrence
Island

Norton Sound

Nulato

Yukon

Manley Hot
Springs

Unalakleet

*Yukon
Delta*

Mountain Village

Yukon

Moose Creek

DENALI
NATIONAL PARK
AND PRESERVE

Camp
Denali

Kuskokwim

Mt. McKinley (Denali)
20,320 ft.

CHAPTER 4

A L A S K A

③

B E R I N G

St. Matthew
Island

Nunivak
Island

Bethel

K U S K O K W I M   M O U N T A I N S

Chulitna

Talkeetna

S E A

5,500 ft.

Lake
Clark

Kenai

①

Cook

Inlet

Kenai
Peninsula

STERLING HWY.

*Kuskokwim
Bay*

Iliamna Lake

Homer

Kenai

Susitna

Kachemak
Bay

Seldovia

Pribilof
Islands

Dillingham

Augustine Volcano
4,025 ft.

CHAPTER 3

Areas featured in chapters

Selected park or monument

National Forest

Glacier

Ferry

KATMAI
NATIONAL PARK
AND PRESERVE

Hallo Bay

Afognak
Island

B r i s t o l

B a y

Kodiak

Note: Map highlights features
described in this book.

0   50   100   150   200
STATUTE MILES

0   50   100   150   200
KILOMETERS

A L A S K A   P E N I N S U L A

ALASKA MARINE HIGHWAY

Shelikof Strait

Kodiak
Island

L E U T I A N   I S L A N D S

Chignik

Unimak Island

King Cove

Umnak
I.

Unalaska
I.

Unalaska

P A C I F I C

OCEAN

BEAUFORT SEA

NUNAVU

Prudhoe Bay •Kaktovik •Tuktoyaktuk

L O P E   Mackenzie
                   Bay
                                                    Mackenzie River Delta
        E
9,020 ft. +   •Inuvik
                                                        8 CHAPTER 6
   (11)
   DALTON   Tsiigehtchic
   HIGHWAY   (Arctic Red River)
                          Richardson   •Fort McPherson   ARCTIC CIRCLE
      R   Mountains   Mackenzie
      A   Arctic Red
Porcupine   Bell   N O R T H W E S T
      N   Eagle   Eagle
      G   Plains
      E   T E R R I T O R I E S
(2)   Ogilvie
                   Yukon   Ogilvie
Fort   M A C K E N Z I E
Yukon   Mountains TOMBSTONE
                                   5   TERRITORIAL   S E L W Y N   M O U N T A I N S
                                              PARK
   S K A   Blackstone North Fork Pass
                                              4,229 ft.   9,750 ft.+   M O U N T A I N S
(2)   Eagle   9
                                   Dawson   Klondike
(3) •Fairbanks   Peel   Y U K O N   Undefined
     Tanana   Boundary
        (2) ALASKA   Klondike
Mt. Healy   HIGHWAY   Stewart
5,716 ft.   Tok   Pelly
 + Park Entrance (4)   (5)
R A N G E   (1)   (2)   Yukon
DENALI   (1)   KLONDIKE
PARK   Glennallen   HIGHWAY   ALASKA   HIGHWAY
PARKS ROAD
HIGHWAY   WRANGELL–ST. ELIAS   Kluane   Liard
                           NATIONAL PARK   Lake   ★Whitehorse
          •Palmer   Copper   16,421 ft.+   Kluane   Aishihik
13,176 ft.+ CHUGACH   Chitina AND PRESERVE   1   NATIONAL   Kathleen   Teslin
•Anchorage MOUNTAINS   CHAPTER 5   PARK   Sheep Mt. Lake   Lake
CHUGACH NATIONAL FOREST   KLUANE   AND RESERVE + Kathleen
  •Valdez   NATIONAL   Haines   Tatshenshini   B R I T I S H
•Whittier Prince   •Cordova   PARK   Mt. Logan Junction River   Atlin
Mountains William   Copper   AND RESERVE   19,551 ft. HAINES   Dalton   Lake
•Seward   Sound   River   CHAPTER 2   ST. HWY.   Post
           Orca   Delta   E L I A S •Skagway
           Inlet   Kluane   Tatshenshini-Alsek
KENAI FJORDS COPPER   Icefields   PROVINCIAL
NATIONAL PARK RIVER   PARK   Haines   C O A S T
              HIGHWAY   Yakutat   Alsek River   M O U N T A I N S
         GULF OF ALASKA Bay   •Yakutat
                         Dry Bay   GLACIER BAY   C O L U M B I A
                         Mt. Fairweather +   NATIONAL PARK
                         15,300 ft.   AND PRESERVE   ★Juneau
                                                     TONGASS   UNITED STATES
                                                                CANADA
                                                     Chichagof Admiralty   +10,035 ft.
                                                     Island   Island
                                                     N A T I O N A L
                                                     •Sitka   Baranof Kupreanof •Petersburg
                                                     Kruzof Island Island Mitkof I. M O U N T A I N S
                                                     St. Lazaria Islands Sitka Sound •Wrangell
                                                     Sound
                                                     F O R E S T   Revillagigedo
                                                     A L E X A N D E R   TOTEM Island
                                                                              BIGHT
                                                     ALASKA MARINE HIGHWAY   S.H.P. MISTY FJORDS
                                                     Prince of Wales Ketchikan• NATIONAL MONUMENT
                                                     Island
                                                     A R C H I P E L A G O   •Metlakatla
                                                                     CHAPTER 1
                                                                              •Prince
                                                                              Rupert
                                      Dixon Entrance

O C E A N   Graham
                                                             QUEEN   Island
                                                             CHARLOTTE
                                                             ISLANDS

ARCTIC OCEAN

RUSSIA   ALASKA   CANADA
                (U.S.)

Bering Sea

Attu I.

Aleutian Islands   PACIFIC OCEAN

Traveling
THE MARINE HIGHWAY

Smooth water invites travelers into the wilds of Misty Fiords National Monument in Southeast Alaska.

Graceful flukes shed a sheet of water as a humpback whale dives into the waters of Southeast Alaska's Frederick Sound.

TRAVELING THE MARINE HIGHWAY
Southeastern Alaska and the Inside Passage

G AZING DOWN FROM THE PLANE AS IT APPROACHED KETCHIKAN, I could see that the town existed in emphatic remoteness on its island home at the southern end of Alaska's panhandle. It was an outpost of civilization surrounded by thousands of square miles of mountains and forests and a maze of inlets, channels, coves, and other backwaters of the Pacific. Like almost all the towns and villages of Southeast Alaska, it can be reached only by boat or plane. No roads connect Ketchikan to the outside.

The Southeast's isolation stems largely from its geography. Consisting of a coastal strip and associated islands, measuring about 400 miles from north to south and up to 150 miles east to west, the panhandle runs along the extreme northwest corner of British Columbia. The 5,000- to 10,000-foot crest of the Coast Mountains, a forbidding barrier almost impossible to cross, roughly forms the border between Southeast Alaska and B.C.

As I exited the airport terminal, a cool drizzle licked my face. Ah, the traditional Ketchikan greeting. Sort of Southeast Alaska's equivalent of being welcomed at the Honolulu airport with a lei. To be fair, during the summer the Alaska sun does shine fairly often, but Ketchikan is indeed one of the wettest spots on the continent. For many residents, brown rubber boots—variously known as Ketchikan sneakers, Sitka slippers, and Alaska tennis shoes—are de rigueur. Practicality trumps fashion in a place that splashes around in 150 inches of rain a year. Of course, not all of the Southeast gets so much precipitation (known as "liquid sunshine" to locals). Some places record a mere 80 inches a year—still enough to support the temperate rain forest that blankets the panhandle.

Shortly after arriving in downtown Ketchikan, I did as the locals do when it's raining: I donned my rain gear and went about my business. (Left the umbrella at home, though, for I knew well that in the Southeast it's viewed as a foppish affectation, only slightly less ridiculous than a bow tie.) I began my exploration along the water-front promenade, where the cruise ships pull in. Because it was mid-May, no ships were tied at the dock, but by early June the 2,000-passenger leviathans would loom above the waterfront nearly every day, disgorging hordes of daytrippers. As I strolled the promenade and nearby streets, I encountered dozens of stores aimed at the cruise-ship crowd, ranging from places offering T-shirts emblazoned with images of roaring bears to swanky boutiques selling luxurious fur coats. Jewelry and diamond stores were strangely abundant.

The commercial spawn of the cruise-ship boom have malled downtown Ketchikan to some extent. But there's also a positive side to the changes, on top of the fact that the town has needed tourism dollars since the decline of the timber industry, long Ketchikan's economic mainstay. Amid the made-in-China souvenirs and the absen-tee-owner diamond marts are numerous worthwhile locally owned and operated shops, such as the idiosyncratic Soho Coho Gallery and Gift Store.

Soho Coho operates in a refurbished early-1900s dance hall on Creek Street, the old red-light district, now a pedestrians-only boardwalk above Ketchikan Creek. The creek's cold, clear waters provide spawning grounds for four species of salmon during the summer, and a hoary Ketchikan joke refers to Creek Street as "the only place where both men and salmon head upstream to spawn."

The salmon are not incidental to Soho Coho. The gallery owner, Ray Troll, produces what he calls "fin art," a fishy branch of fine art. A former cannery worker who came to Ketchikan decades ago to help his sister run a seafood store, Troll is unabashedly obsessed with fish. He draws and paints fanciful and funny images, such as his famous "Spawn 'Til You Die" creation: a familiar skull and crossbones, except the crossbones are salmon. Troll also seriously—as seriously as his wry personality allows—studies fossil fish and makes art of them. Take his depiction of *Leedichthys*, a Jurassic fish the size of a blue whale. In one drawing he rendered it in great detail, but pictured it flying across an Alaskan skyline.

Troll's combination of artistic talent and scientific interest has resulted in big traveling exhibits that have made the rounds of major art and science museums. Yet this success has not changed his downhome attitude or goofy sensibility. Browsing in Soho Coho, I got the strong impression that Troll takes just as much pleasure in putting his fin art on T-shirts, caps, playing cards, and other everyday objects. I suspect he doesn't mind reeling in some of those tourist dollars. But that works out well for the tourists, too. Instead of buying some T-shirt stamped with a cookie-cutter image of a moose, they can take home a shirt that shows a fierce salmon sporting a beard and turban with the words, "Wanted Dead or Alive, O Salmon Bin Laden."

I spent one morning in Ketchikan having a great time not going to Misty Fiords National Monument. Sure, I'd rather have climbed aboard the floatplane on which I'd reserved space and flown over the 2.3-million-acre monument. I yearned to see the mountains, the lush temperate rain forest, the glaciers, the wildlife, and the waterfalls showering over 2,000-foot cliffs into the sea. But the place isn't called *Misty* Fiords for nothing. On occasion the rain and fog get so thick that even veteran pilots, like the guys at Southeast Aviation, won't risk flying. Veteran pilots in particular won't risk it; they know the old saying: There are old pilots, and there are bold pilots, but there are no old, bold pilots.

While we were waiting around, hoping that the mist would lift, I enjoyed hanging out and drinking coffee with a couple of the pilots. Jerry Scudero, one of Southeast Aviation's co-owners, told of a time he flew his young son out to Misty Fiords. He described the snow on the mountains and the bald eagles flapping across the channels. He landed his floatplane on one of those channels and taxied over to a small beach beneath the cliffs, where he and his son spotted a bear.

Scudero smiled as he recalled his son turning to him and saying, "Man, Dad, that's Alaska."

FROM KETCHIKAN I HEADED NORTH ON ONE OF THE FERRIES OF THE ALASKA Marine Highway, the circulatory system of the Southeast. These "blue canoes" serve much of the state's west coast, but nowhere are they more numerous and more essential than in the panhandle. The ferries haul high school basketball teams to their away games; residents of small villages to the larger towns on shopping expeditions ("larger" meaning a place like Ketchikan, population 8,000); grandparents going to visit grandchildren; kids going on field trips; and salesmen calling on far-flung customers.

"It's like a floating city, with its own water, sewage, security, and everything," said Lavena Sargent. Sargent was the purser—the ship's officer in charge of accounts—on one of the ferries I rode during my travels in Southeast Alaska. An affable, crisply efficient woman, she had worked on the ferries for many years. "This is the most fun I've had in my entire life," she said, citing events like the many weddings she had seen on board. She told me that five times on her ferry watch, babies have been born. "There are a few 'Malaspinas' running around out there," she said, referring to kids who had the misfortune to be born on the ferry of that name and whose impressionable parents didn't consult a baby names book any further.

"It's hard to imagine how much this ferry is a lifeline," said Sargent. As a simple example, she pointed out that the ferries regularly tote fresh fruit and vegetables from Washington to Southeast communities that freighters can't reach because they can't squeeze through the narrow channels. More seriously, 10 or 20 times a year one of the ferries gets an emergency call and goes to the aid of a distressed ship.

A tour boat takes a lucky band of passengers

into Misty Fiords National Monument on a mist-less day.

With several hundred passengers onboard at any given time, the human comedy never ceases. Sargent said that every year there are locals who take the ferry not to get anywhere but just to have a place to do their taxes without the distractions of home. Stowaways pop up now and then. Sargent's most memorable was a man who had escaped from a mental hospital; he kept asking them to turn off the radar so he wouldn't receive signals from the Martians. Finally, there are the tourists who think Alaska is as foreign as, well, Mars. Sometimes travelers—American travelers—come up to Sargent and ask if she or any crew members speak English, or if they use American dollars in Alaska. Some of these urban types have asked Sargent when they feed the whales and have urged her to get someone to clean the debris off the glaciers.

AS THE FERRY PULLED AWAY FROM KETCHIKAN THAT SUNNY AFTERNOON, I stood on the stern deck and watched as the forest and mountains swallowed the receding town. A woman joined me at the railing and made small talk for about ten seconds before, impatient with pride, she pointed at another ferry trailing about half a mile behind us and told me that one of her nephews was its newly appointed captain and another nephew its purser. She explained that it was a smaller ship than the one on which we stood and that it served the Southeast's smaller communities.

Once that proud aunt moved on (not 30 seconds later I overheard her telling an elderly couple about her nephews), I leaned on the top rail and watched the shore with the mountains rising steeply behind it as we cruised northwest up Tongass Narrows. Actually, I watched both shores: From each side the land leans in close, for the channel measures only about half a mile across. Later that day the ship's purser told me that Tongass Narrows was nothing—Wrangell Narrows, he said, now there was a tight passage. He told me that in Wrangell Narrows a person standing on the ship could take two rocks and throw them, one to the west and one to the east, and hit land with both. I came to regret that he'd ever told me that.

From the railing on the upper deck I stared at the dark green wall of the temperate rain forest, the tall conifers and the riot of vegetation that makes the understory so thick you'd want a machete to move through it. I remembered bushwhacking through such a forest once—sans machete—and covering only half a mile in two hours of strenuous hiking. I much preferred eyeing it from a passing ship. Most people think rain forest only exists in the tropics, but a thin sliver grows on the west coast of North America, from far northern California to southern Alaska. Of course, the suite of plant and animal species is very different in Alaska compared with the Amazon—black bears instead of jaguars and spruce instead of kapok trees—but each type of rain forest confronts visitors with an awesome profusion of life.

After an hour or so of enjoying the forest and the occasional bald eagle and waterfall, I headed downstairs to check out the ferry. I wandered through the forward

In the wet climate of Misty Fiords National Monument,
moss grows on everything, including this decomposing boardwalk.
This tract of temperate rain forest near Ketchikan gets drenched
by more than 150 inches of rain annually.

The boldly colored figures on totem poles hold great cultural

and historical meaning for Alaska natives in the Southeast.

lounge, which was about half full. By June, it'd be jammed. People in the window seats gazed at the scenery. Others sat at tables reading, playing cards, chatting, sleeping. On one of the covered decks some passengers had pitched their tents, creating a little campground—campfires strictly forbidden, however. I drifted by the cocktail lounge, where a couple of passengers sat on bar stools, drinking beneath a flamboyant velvet painting of Elvis, awful even by the standards of that notorious medium.

After 10 or 15 minutes I started feeling itchy to get out on deck again, afraid I'd miss something. I took the nearest door and walked onto the upper front deck. No sooner had I reached the railing than I saw a spout. A whale exhalation. A young guy standing near me yelled, "Did you see that?" I assured him I had indeed seen the ten-foot-high steam puff. I saw the next one, too, and the next, and then a spout that was only about a hundred yards off the starboard bow. I cursed that I'd left my binoculars below, but the guy graciously handed me his for a look. As I focused on the vicinity of the last blow, the whale surfaced, raised its tail, and swung it down forcefully into the water. And again, and again, and again. This behavior is known as lobtailing, and when the tail being slapped belongs to a 50-foot, 40-ton behemoth, the splashes are impressive.

Judging by the graceful shape and enormous size of the flukes (the wing shapes on either side of the end of the tail), I guessed that our whale was a humpback. But I didn't have to guess for long, because moments later the whale breached, heaving its body almost completely out of the water and twisting in the air before coming down onto the surface with a thunderous whomp.

Whale researchers say that on a quiet day you can hear the splash from the reentry of a breaching humpback from several miles away. While the whale was airborne, I noted its long, slender flippers, perhaps 15 feet from base to tip—proportionately the longest of any whale and a dead giveaway that it was a humpback. Marine biologists hypothesize that whales breach in order to get an aerial view, to dislodge parasites, to signal to their running mates via the loud splash—or, say some cetologists, just to have some fun. If the latter is correct, this whale was having a hell of a good time. It continued breaching and lobtailing until the ferry had left it so far behind that it faded into the horizon.

HALF A DAY AFTER BOARDING, I GOT OFF THE FERRY IN WRANGELL, A TOWN AT the northern tip of Wrangell Island, about 85 as-the-crow-flies miles north of Ketchikan. This fishing and logging community of 2,200 souls is one of the smallest ports on the main line of the marine highway, and the large cruise ships seldom come here. Oddly, though, commercial jets fly in twice daily.

As I wandered the tidy little downtown of Wrangell, I saw a hardware store, some down-home cafés, a quilting supplies shop, the newspaper office, a drugstore, the

Elks Hall, a grocery store, and other businesses oriented to the locals, with only a few souvenir shops and none of the diamond marts prevalent in the cruise ship ports. One resident told me that Wrangell is the kind of place where 90 percent of the population turns out for the town's Fourth of July parade and festivities.

Grandma's Barber Shop, a little downtown hole-in-the-wall, epitomizes the town's friendly, laid-back character. Grandma, aka Clara Haley, is an older but vital woman with long gray hair who has been barbering in Wrangell for years. Because she works limited hours, she keeps a sign-up board outside the shop. That way, even when the shop is closed, customers can claim one of her 15-minute slots. You might assume that she limits her work hours due to her age, but I suspect she's out doing other things. I suspect this because I saw a blackboard hanging in a nearby shop window, listing the current leaders of the Wrangell King Salmon Derby. Number 10 on the list was Clara Haley, who had landed a 26.7-pounder. I'm guessing that when she's not at the barber shop, Grandma's out fishing, looking to move up the leader board.

One blustery afternoon I rented a bike and headed out on a two-wheeled tour. About a mile from the ferry dock at the north end of town, I stopped at Petroglyph Beach, where I wandered along the shore and discovered a number of the old rock carvings that give this beach its name. The age and origin of these stylized impressions of killer whales, human figures, and birds remain a mystery, but experts think that the artists are ancestors of the Tlingit, the native people who currently inhabit the area.

I ran my fingertips across the deeply etched figures, but I did so delicately, not wanting to hasten the erosion of these stone echoes of an ancient way of life. I found more modern evidence of Tlingit culture on Chief Shakes Island, connected to downtown by a footbridge. I admired the authentic 1939 replica of a Tlingit clan house and the totem poles. While I was gazing upon the brooding raven figure at the top of one pole, I noticed that by coincidence several live ravens occupied the tree branches just a few feet above their cedar likeness.

My bike lay outside the Wrangell Museum for well over an hour. Opened in 2004, this spacious new museum houses collections of such number and quality that it seems to belong in a city ten times the size of Wrangell. The entrance is graced by four carved wooden house posts, Tlingit treasures from the 1700s that are thought to be the oldest of such posts surviving in Alaska. Many of the displays relate to the area's native history, from inhabitants dating back 10,000 years to the contemporary Tlingit.

I also enjoyed the exhibits depicting the rowdy gold rush days. For ten days in late 1890s, Wyatt Earp filled in as deputy marshal and tried to tame the town. One time he took a pistol away from a disorderly man only to recognize him as a fellow he had arrested 20 years earlier in Dodge City. Reporting on Wrangell in the January 1899 issue of NATIONAL GEOGRAPHIC, a writer described that "a score of saloons ran wide open" and that "the most barefaced gambling games and swindling schemes were conducted on every side without concealment." Summing up, the author concluded that "this 'boomtown' of 6,000 inhabitants displayed all the worst features of such lapses in civilization." By comparison, Wrangell's got a handle on its outlaw element today.

*The forested mountains that frame Juneau account in part for its reputation
as the most scenic state capital in the United States. Five minutes
from the downtown government offices lies wild country, populated by bears
instead of lobbyists—you decide which are more dangerous.*

MYRIAD OUTDOOR ADVENTURES BECKON IN THE WRANGELL AREA, BUT the big dog is the Stikine River, the mouth of which lies only four or five miles from downtown. The fastest-flowing navigable river in North America, the Stikine rises deep in British Columbia and races 330 miles down from the Canadian mountains to the Inside Passage, the final 30 miles running through Alaska. A few hardy rafters and kayakers make the run from B.C., but most visitors—locals and travelers—start in town and go upriver by powerboat to begin their river adventure.

I went up the Stikine with Eric Yancey, owner and operator of an ecotourism outfit and the man who pioneered these river trips in the late 1980s. His experience came in handy as soon as we were out of the harbor, as he navigated through the sandbars of the huge delta, a stopover for hundreds of thousands of migrating shorebirds and water-fowl. As we started up the river proper, we spotted an active bald eagle nest. In the spring, hundreds of baldies congregate here to feed on a big run of hooligan (also called smelter candlefish), as do Steller sea lions.

Soon the river fractured into multiple channels, and we veered into a sinuous passage that at times measured only about 25 feet across, with willows and cottonwoods arching over the water. We saw a moose disappearing into a thicket. Yancey told me that once his tour had come across a wobbly-legged moose calf that had been born so recently it was still steaming. After a mile or two Yancey eased us up Andrew Creek, a clear-water stream that empties into the glacier-silt brown of the Stikine. In July a nice run of king salmon heads up the creek to spawn. Yancey carries fishing gear for anyone who wants to try to hook some dinner.

Back on one of the river channels, we entered a series of tight S-curves. As we puttered along, Yancey looked at me with a mischievous smile and asked if I'd like to see what his custom-made jet boat could do.

I nodded.

Now, before I go any further, let's get something straight. I think that generally people shouldn't go hot-rodding around the great outdoors in loud motorized vehicles. While cross-country skiing in Yellowstone one winter, I just about had my eardrums shattered by a pack of snowmobiles that roared by, scaring the scat out of all the wildlife within a five-mile radius. I've had a tranquil afternoon in the Oregon sand dunes ruined by the dentist-drill shrilling of all-terrain vehicles doing doughnuts in the fragile dune vegetation. Once when I was exploring the Everglades, a quartet of high-decibel jet skis revved down the previously still backwater channel, scattering gators and egrets in their wake. So what happened on the Stikine was not an endorsement of such behavior. Let's just say I had a momentary lapse.

As I was saying ... I nodded. Yancey's smile widened into a grin, and he opened up the throttle, unleashing the jet in that jet boat. In moments we were powering along at more than 30 miles per hour, leaning through the S-curve turns like ski racers on a slalom course, shouldering around the gates. I guess I ought to claim that I didn't enjoy the ride, but I don't think I should heap dishonesty on top of my hypocrisy, so I have to say, *Yeehaw!*

Slowing down to cruising speed, we continued upriver for several miles to Chief Shakes Hot Springs, where the Forest Service has built two hot tubs, one indoors and one outside in a meadow at the edge of the forest. The water bubbling up from underground is so hot that they have to pipe in cold water to cool it, so people can bask rather than boil.

Just around the bend is the entrance to Shakes Lake, a five-mile-long finger of water that leads through towering mountains to Shakes Glacier. As we nosed up the lake we spied a black bear on the shore about one hundred feet away, a common sighting around the lake. Mountain goats also frequent the area, but we didn't see any that day. We continued another couple of miles but ended up stopping well short of the glacier because we were in a comfy 28-foot tour boat and not in a massive Coast Guard icebreaker. Yancey had predicted that our mid-May venture would encounter ice, but he hadn't mentioned how wondrous it would be.

Yancey cut the engine and we drifted quietly. I could hear the thin ice at the edge of the frozen surface breaking up as the backwash from our boat gently swelled beneath it. It made a resonant, musical sound, like wind chimes tinkling in a soft breeze. The sun bore down on the small icebergs floating around us, igniting the infinite shades of radiant blue characteristic of dense glacial ice. Raising my gaze a few degrees, I took in the cascades rushing down the mountain slopes and diving over sheer cliffs into the lake. A closer look at the dark stone of those cliffs revealed ancient scars left by the grinding of the Chief Shakes Glacier back when the frozen river of ice, raspy with silt and rocks it had picked up along the way, had slowly pushed across the land where the lake rests today. Yancey and I sat silently for a while, savoring a realm that changed every minute and yet was the same in its essence as it had been for thousands of years.

Just before boarding the ferry out of Wrangell, I picked up half a dozen rocks suitable for throwing. I'd remembered the purser's claim about Wrangell Narrows, and I intended to put it to the test. An hour and a half later, the ferry slowed dramatically and executed a strange, almost right-angle turn to enter the Narrows, a constricted, 15-mile-long channel that squeezes between Mitkof and Kupreanof Islands. Centering between red and green buoys, the ship proceeded through a series of sharp-angled turns.

I ducked out of sight into a passageway and began swinging my right arm in big circles, like a relief pitcher warming up. As the ship eased through the narrowest stretch, I stepped up to the starboard railing, glanced around to make sure no one was looking, and let fly.

Like all the other towns of Southeast Alaska, Sitka is a seafaring community.
Commercial fishing boats, charter boats, sportfishing boats, tour boats, rowboats,
water taxis, kayaks, canoes... There's even a semisubmersible that takes its passengers
underwater. Some locals claim that there are more boats than households in town.

Dungeness crabs are just one part of the multifaceted fishing industry of Petersburg, Alaska.
Fifty million pounds of fish are hauled aboard each year by Petersburg fishers.
Most are salmon, supplemented by halibut, black cod, herring, crabs, and
other nonfish species such as sea cucumbers, abalone, and sea urchins.

The rock arced toward the looming shore but fell maybe a hundred feet short. I tried again, harder, hard enough to hurt my arm, but the rock still fell some 50 feet short. One more painful heave, but still a jeering splash 50 feet from the shore. Looking to salvage half a success, I ran across to the port railing and tried three throws at that shore. Same story—nothing but a sore arm.

But my failure didn't discredit the purser's claim about someone being able to hit both shores with rocks. He just forgot to mention that the someone has to be a major league outfielder. As I stood there, simultaneously massaging my aching arm and appreciating the forest and mountains that hugged the ship, I overheard a woman standing near me say to her companion, "You'd think you'd get tired of the scenery, but I haven't found that to be true."

We stopped briefly in the fishing town of Petersburg, at the north end of Wrangell Narrows, and then moved northwest up Frederick Sound. Known for its marine life, the sound didn't disappoint; I saw several humpback whales and innumerable Dall's porpoises, sleek marine mammals that are coal-black with a white patch on their flanks. Once a few of these playful critters swam over and spent several minutes riding our ferry's bow wave.

Relishing the sunny weather, I hung around on one deck or another for several hours, but I'd been up since 3 a.m. and, wildlife and sunshine notwithstanding, my fatigue finally told me it was time to take a nap. Unfortunately, I'd gotten an inside cabin, meaning no window. On my previous trip I'd been in an outside cabin and had been able to gaze out the window while lying in the upper bunk. Sweet. But a word of caution about upper bunks. This time around, lying in my bunk, I noticed that the metal ceiling, a mere two feet above my face, had a skull-shaped dent in it. A previous occupant must have awakened and sat up before remembering where he was.

Traveling in the viewless inside cabin was akin to visiting the Louvre blindfolded. I kept wondering what I was missing, so I ended up spending little time there except when asleep. I decided that I preferred the third—and much cheaper—accommodation option of no cabin, which is the way I traveled on subsequent legs of my ferry journey through the Southeast. The many passengers who go cabinless find all sorts of places to sleep. One time I simply slept in a reclining chair, which was okay if you're not prone to getting a stiff neck. Another time I crashed on the floor of the room where they showed movies. That actually was pretty comfortable, and the carpeted surface wasn't sticky with spilled sodas as a regular theater would be. The fact is, this ferry crew is pretty laissez-faire about sleeping arrangements, as long as you're out of the way and safe.

I GOT OFF THE FERRY IN SITKA. THOUGH THE ROUTE I HAD TAKEN WAS classic Inside Passage, winding tortuously through a jumble of islands before reaching

Sea Life Discovery, *a semisubmersible, gives visitors*

underwater views of life beneath the surface of Sitka Sound.

During the summer, passengers set up tents

on the decks of the ferries that ply the Inside Passage.

the Sitka dock some 120 miles northwest of Wrangell, the town itself is the one mainline port that faces the open Pacific. The town site on the west side of Baranof Island is only partly shielded from the open ocean by Kruzof Island, about ten miles to the west, and a scattering of smaller islands.

Sitka's celebrated setting lived up to its reputation: the 4,000-foot peaks just to the east; the heavily forested islands to the north; the waters of Sitka Sound and open ocean to the south and southwest; and the volcanic cone of Mount Edgecumbe, about 3,200 feet tall, directly west on the southern tip of Kruzof Island. Drop-dead gorgeous.

This town of 8,800 is almost as appealing as its backdrop, as I discovered when I headed out from my downtown hotel for a walk the next day. The small commercial area is a nice blend of shops, some for tourists and some for locals. One or two big cruise ships hit Sitka most summer days, but the citizens have consciously limited cruise-ship visits by refusing to build a dock big enough to handle those behemoths, which must therefore anchor in the harbor and send people ashore on tenders. Some local growth boosters advocate building a dock for the large cruise ships, but they've been outvoted so far by those whose sentiments are summed up in a bumper sticker I saw around town: "No Pier Pressure."

Restricting the influence of cruise ships has enabled Sitka to retain its small-town informality, which I found endearing. For example, the former school superintendent stages big crab feeds in a parking lot, serving heaps of the Dungeness crabs his fisherman son catches. Or consider Ludwig's, Sitka's best restaurant and one of the finest in all of Alaska. Two women own the place, run the place, and do all the cooking. Ludwig's has only six or eight tables plus a little four-stool wine bar and produces maybe 50 meals a night, but what meals! I indulged in paella Andalucia, most of whose ingredients had recently inhabited the cold ocean waters around Sitka: clams, scallops, calamari, and prawns, with chicken and chorizo sausage served over saffron rice and vegetables. Now and then the chefs would come out and talk to the customers, most of whom were locals. Ludwig's also operates a soup cart out on the street during the day, serving smoked salmon, clam chowder, and the like.

SOMETIMES THE CHARM OF THE PEOPLE WHO INHABIT REMOTE LITTLE TOWNS in a place like Southeast Alaska can cross the line into flaming eccentricity. A reliable source told me of a representative individual who made his home in Skagway, at the northern end of Alaska's panhandle, 164 miles due north from Sitka. This free spirit, named Ed, scratched out a living painting vans. One winter day, without telling anyone, he simply disappeared. But no one thought anything of it because this guy didn't exactly live according to an agenda. Probably just took off to find some sun.

A couple of weeks later, a van drove off the ferry in Skagway and started roaming around town. Skagway is a tiny place where only a few hundred people live in the winter. Almost no one visits during that harsh season, so the townspeople would have noticed any van just driving around. But they especially noticed this one, because in large letters on the side were printed the words "Publisher's Clearing House." The locals figured that the van must be driving around looking for the address of some lucky citizen who'd won a big jackpot. A couple of people jumped in a car and started following the van, trying in vain to see who was inside it behind the darkly tinted windows. Others joined the parade until maybe ten vehicles were lined up behind the van. This mystery tour continued for about half an hour until the van stopped. Everyone watched as the driver's door opened ... and out came Ed. Laughing his head off, no doubt feeling that his elaborate joke was worth the incredible amount of time and trouble he'd devoted to it.

I enjoy the past residents of Southeast Alaska almost as much as such characters from the present. This was especially true in Sitka, where I encountered native Alaska history throughout the town, most notably at the Sheldon Jackson Museum, Alaska's oldest museum and one of its finest. The core of the extensive collection, which comes from all over the state, was gathered in the 19th century by the peripatetic Sheldon Jackson, a missionary who also served as Alaska's first general agent of education. The museum is quartered in what is claimed to be Alaska's first concrete building.

Museum display cases present frightening shaman's masks carved from cedar, body armor made of walrus bone, a dance apron fashioned from porcupine quills, and an Eskimo whaling suit made of *oogruk*—bearded sealskin. The outfit looks like a space suit without the helmet. I marveled at the ability of yesteryear's Alaskan natives to make use of everything in their environment. I'd hate to see the results if my family and I had to fashion our clothes and tools from the rose bushes in our yard and the pelts of neighborhood pets.

When museum fatigue put lead in my legs and made my eyelids droop—it eventually hits me no matter how fascinating I find a museum—I cleared the cobwebs by taking a ride in a submarine. Okay, the *Sea Life Discovery* vessel isn't a full-blown sub, but it comes wonderfully close. The top deck of this semisubmersible stands above the level of the water, while the lower deck, where its 20 or 30 passengers travel, extends about six feet beneath the water's surface. Each passenger sits facing outward, looking through the generous bank of downward-slanted windows. Every seat is the best seat in the house.

As the boat eased above the eelgrass beds of Sitka Sound at the pace of a slow walk, I spotted sunflower stars (mistakenly called starfish) beneath us, two feet in diameter with 20 rays each; platter-sized lion's mane jellyfish drifting past, maybe a hundred wispy tentacles trailing behind them; and bright red rock crabs scuttling across the sun-dappled seafloor.

Already delighted, I became positively entranced when we slipped into the kelp forests, the giant yellow-green algae shimmying in the tide, luminous as the sunlight shone through its translucent, leaflike blades. Sometimes our vessel plowed right through the kelp, and masses of five-foot-long blades wiped slowly across our windows, revealing kelp crabs and colorful shrimp mere inches away as I leaned right up to the window. It's the closest you can get to scuba diving without getting wet.

Having seen what lies beneath, I was eager to see what lies above the surface of fertile Sitka Sound. Many charter outfits run tours, but I was lucky enough to find Capt. Davey Lubin, a perfect match for my tastes. Lubin takes up to six passengers on custom tours. He has worked as a commercial fisherman, a U.S. Forest Service staff member, and a biology teacher. With a B.S. degree in forest science, he knows and loves the natural world in general and the Sitka area in particular.

Almost all the other tour boat captains take people out sportfishing, but Lubin only conducts tours that focus on wildlife and ecology. Maintaining that focus turned out to be easy the day I explored Sitka Sound with him. Lubin, two friends of his, and I motored away from the dock that morning, and before I'd even taken out my binoculars, several bald eagles flapped across the harbor. In another minute, we'd spotted our first sea otter.

A bit later we came across seven sea otters lolling in the canopy of a kelp forest, including a pup sleeping on top of its mother's chest. As we watched, some of the otters began feeding. I saw one dive to the bottom of the shallow cove, surface with a crab, twist, and assume a back-float position. On its back, grasping the crab firmly with its handlike forepaws, it smashed the shellfish against a rock it had balanced on its torso and then picked the delectable meat out of the cracked shell, munching away. So organized was this fellow that I was a little surprised he forgot the cocktail sauce.

In the early afternoon we cut across the mouth of the sound, hoping to spot humpback whales. Later in the season, dozens would gather here, but we only had a fleeting glimpse of one. No matter, for we soon arrived at the St. Lazaria Islands, part of the Alaska Maritime National Wildlife Refuge. Though little more than a few massive rocks, covered with grass and trees and jutting from the water off the southern tip of Kruzof Island, this refuge hosts nearly a million nesting seabirds during the summer, including kittiwakes, murres, cormorants, and crowd-pleasing puffins. As with the whales, we were too early in the year for big numbers, but we saw thousands of birds swirling overhead, like a storm of wind-driven autumn leaves.

As we headed back toward the harbor, Lubin and one of his friends exchanged impish glances, and Lubin shoved a cassette tape into his sound system. Sea chanteys. Naturally. Lubin and his friend proceeded to sing along with more enthusiasm than skill.

The tape ended, and we continued in silence for a while. Having amply displayed his goofy side, Lubin revealed he could be serious, too. He spoke about the profound pleasure he takes in showing people the scenery and wildlife of Sitka Sound and in explaining its ecological intricacies. He said that some of his customers are so "starved for wildness," as he put it, that beholding the mountains and the whales, the bears and the forest, the sea otters and the bird colonies overwhelms them, and they end up crying—presumably crying for joy as they experience the sublime wildness that lies at the heart of Southeast Alaska. ∎

The Davidson Glacier, near Haines, is one of the dozens of glaciers in Southeast
Alaska. Some of these rivers of ice grind down from coastal mountains
all the way to the waters of the Inside Passage, where great hunks of ice split off
from the faces of the glaciers and belly flop into the sea.

The rugged Coast Range Mountains discourage the construction of roads between British

Columbia and Southeast Alaska, preserving the remoteness of the region.

Majesty in detail

Southeast Alaska is a big land. It's easy to become

mesmerized by the panoramic views of

mountains, rivers, forests, islands, and the sea.

But reserve some time for close-ups,

for kneeling down to appreciate the details.

Much beauty and wonder exists in

the feather, the leaf, the stone, and the track.

Sometimes paying attention to details has practical value. For example, an examination of understory plants in the rain forest might yield a mouthful of savory huckleberries or salmonberries. Knowing how to identify Southeast Alaska's many wild berries also could save your life. Consider the baneberry, shown on page 40: These cherry-red beauties are highly poisonous to humans.

Scientists, whether professional or amateur, thrive on details. When a house-size hunk of ice splits off from a tidewater glacier and crashes into the sea, it requires no knowledge to behold this spectacular event and exclaim "Wow!"

But between "Wow!" moments, clued-in onlookers can discern the nature of the passing icebergs by noting their colors. The bluer a berg, the denser its ice. A white berg has large numbers of air bubbles trapped inside it; and a greenish-black berg calved off the bottom of a glacier.

As with berries and icebergs, the details of an animal's appearance provide lots of information. The fact that a bald eagle, right, lacks the signature white head tells you that the bird is immature. Baldies don't get all their adult features, such as the white head, white tail, and yellow beak, until their fourth or fifth year.

The details of an animal's behavior can also be revealing. If you see a bald eagle engaging in piracy, even if you're too far away to see the color of its head, it's probably immature. The juveniles like to harass crows and other birds that are carrying fish. They keep at it until their victims drop the catch, which the young eagles then retrieve and devour.

CHAPTER TWO

No road to
THESE GRAND LANDS

Choosing silence over his motor's roar, a lone boater rows through the still waters of the Copper River Delta.

Check out the eccentric signs—especially that of the Alaskan Hotel Bar—on First Street, Cordova's main drag.

NO ROAD TO THESE GRAND LANDS

Cordova and the Copper River Delta

NO ROAD GOES TO CORDOVA AND THE COPPER RIVER DELTA. THAT'S WHY I was on a ferry cruising through Orca Bay toward the eastern end of Prince William Sound, a 50-by-100-mile body of water that is sheltered from the stormy Gulf of Alaska by a bulwark of islands. We'd left Valdez and the Alaskan road system five hours earlier, and during all that time about the only signs of development I'd spotted were a cabin here and a navigation marker there. What I had seen in abundance were glaciers, porpoises, waterfalls, sea otters, sea lions, steep mountains, bald eagles, and just about every imaginable shade of green emanating from the lush rain forest.

On that lightly overcast afternoon in early June, the ferry carried only a few dozen passengers, most of whom looked like locals; Cordova is not a big tourist destination. It is big in one area, though: commercial fishing. More than a third of Cordova's residents fish or work at the town's seafood processing plants, and almost all the other businesses in town, from the marine supplies store to the taco stand, feed off the fishing industry. For much of April and May the ferry had been jammed with thousands of seasonal employees heading for Cordova to work on the boats or in the processing plants during the busy spring and summer fishing season. The town's population of about 2,500 quadruples at the height of the fishing frenzy.

At the head of Orca Bay, the ferry made a 90-degree turn to the south, into Orca Inlet. As you may have guessed, orcas—*Orcinus orca*, the so-called killer whale—inhabit these waters, though none knifed into view that day. In a few minutes the northern edge of Cordova appeared, starting with the ferry dock. Just beyond it were several other piers stacked with red and blue shipping containers, and on the land just behind them stood warehouses and sheds. Nary a trendy waterfront restaurant in sight. My first impression was of a working town.

That was my second and final impression, too. The point was driven home that evening as I ambled around the downtown and the waterfront, which blend together in a five-by-five-block area. In the driveways of houses I saw hard-used pickups and fishing nets laid out for mending. Many of the people walking around town wore rubber boots and heavy-duty rain gear, as if they'd just stepped off a gillnetter or were just about to step onto one. Around nine that night I was passing by Silver Lining Seafoods, down by the harbor, when its doors opened and dozens of people working the evening shift poured out for a break, many wearing aprons stained with fish blood. At one point as I walked down aptly named Seafood Street, I noticed a few men and women smoking and talking as they hung out next to a couple of large buildings that looked as if they'd once been warehouses. Later I learned that these were bunkhouses for seasonal workers.

The harbor itself, the heart of any fishing town, told me something about the essence of Cordova. I saw hundreds of boats tied up to the network of piers, and nothing but boats—no ships, no 120-foot corporate-fleet-sized trawlers. The 25-, 30-, and 35-foot boats I saw are the tools of independent fishers, men and women and families who live in Cordova and operate on their own or maybe with one or two hired crew members during the high season. They do all right, too. In 2004 Cordova ranked 22nd among American ports in terms of the value of its fish catch. Pretty impressive for a tiny, out-of-the-way town, but it doesn't answer the key question that a prospective traveler would ask: Other than to buy a crate of salmon, why would anyone visit this fish-centric backwater? There are plenty of other scenic places in Alaska that are a lot easier to reach.

Indeed, Cordova is not for everyone, as its Chamber of Commerce admits. People looking for urban amenities, fancy resorts, or high-toned small towns, such as Carmel or Aspen, shouldn't bother coming. Neither should travelers who are addicted to McDonald's, Wal-Mart, Starbucks, and all the other familiar chains; Cordova's independent character hasn't been eroded by clone stores (though there is a RadioShack in the local drugstore.) Visitors also won't find much in the way of ready-made attractions, such as major museums, cultural performances, or tourist shops. Cordova does have several small hotels, maybe a dozen B&Bs, an ecotourism resort, and a modest museum, but they aren't what motivates someone to go to all the trouble to get here. Travelers seek out Cordova to get a taste of life in a beyond-the-end-of-the-road Alaskan town.

And the best way to get some of that taste is to talk to the people. They're friendly, genuine, and lively. (Come in February for the Ice Worm Festival and you'll see what I mean by lively.) Strike up a conversation in one of the cafés or bars, and you'll likely gain insight into a way of life that is foreign to most contemporary Americans.

You also will hear some great stories. These fishers have plenty of tales to tell, and not only about the big one that got away. For example, many of the locals have bear stories, since lots of grizzlies and black bears inhabit the forest that breathes down the back of Cordova's neck. I heard several hair-raising accounts, including a classic from Bob Behrends, the recreation program manager for the U.S. Forest Service's Cordova District.

One day he was out in the forest with a colleague planning some trail work when they ran into a grizzly sow and her cub. The cub unfortunately scooted up a tree near Behrends and his friend, so the protective mom charged them. Behrends pumped a shell into the chamber of his shotgun, which Forest Service employees are required to carry when they're doing field work, and drew a bead on the rushing sow. He waited to pull the trigger, however, because grizzlies usually bluff charge. True to form, the big bear stopped about 10 feet short—maybe 20 claw-lengths—and began swaying back and forth. Keeping the shotgun trained on the bear, Behrends glanced to the side to see how his unarmed friend was doing. But his friend wasn't there. Looking around, Behrends spotted his colleague about 20 feet up a nearby tree (not the tree with the cub in it). Eyes back on the bear, Behrends spoke as calmly as he could to the agitated mother, saying that he didn't want to hurt her. Finally, the bear took a few steps toward the tree in which the cub had sought refuge, and Behrends backed off until he was under his colleague. The bear woofed, the cub came down, and off they went. Behrends didn't have to woof; his colleague hurried down and off they went—in the opposite direction from the bears.

THE FRIENDLY HABITS OF CORDOVA RESIDENTS INCLUDE THEIR GENEROSITY. In talking with locals I heard again and again about the exquisite character of the salmon that spawn in the Copper River, especially the sockeyes and kings, the aristocrats of the local fishery. These wild salmon are increasingly prized by chefs and connoisseurs around the world. A local fisherman told me that the savory flavor and high nutritional value of Copper River salmon stem in part from the fact that they're long-distance migrants that swim as far as 150 miles up the river and its tributaries to spawn. Salmon stop eating when they come in from the ocean and start upstream to their spawning grounds, so prior to that grueling journey they store up those tasty fats for which salmon are known. The longer the migration that awaits them, the more their bodies store up, so Copper River salmon are loaded by the time they reach the delta, where the Cordova fishers net them. A local fisheries biologist added that the delta salmon are chock-full of healthful fats because the Copper River discharges a huge amount of nutrients, which feeds vast plankton blooms that in turn enrich the whole food web.

To say I was eager to taste these famed fish would be a gross understatement: I've been known to eat cold leftover salmon for breakfast. As soon as possible after arriving in Cordova I set out to buy an oven-mitt-size fillet of Copper River sockeye and cook it in my room, which had a kitchen. Tragically, however, the seafood companies that have retail outlets were closed. Looking for advice, I walked up to First Street, Cordova's main commercial drag, and ducked into the first open business I encountered, which turned

The backwaters and wetlands of the Copper River Delta harbor a rich array of wildlife

and provide the nursery for the fish that keep the Cordova economy humming.

out to be Orca Books. I explained my quest to the proprietor, but he said, alas, there wasn't any place open that could fill my need. Moved by my plight, he went into his back room to see what he could give me. A happy ending? Not quite yet. His freezer stash, sadly, contained no salmon. But it was the thought that counted. Incidentally, I found out the next day that he was Kelly Weaverling, a former mayor of Cordova.

The story did eventually get around to its happy ending. Taking no chances, I got to one of those retail outlets early the next day and bought an enormous fillet, which I cooked that evening. It was two inches thick and so long that it spilled over the rim of my 12-inch frying pan. I sat at my table overlooking the harbor, watched the boats coming into their slips for the night, and ate every molecule of that slab of sockeye. And, truly, though I didn't add so much as a squeeze of lime juice, that salmon was the finest I've ever tasted.

One afternoon while I was strolling down First Street, I witnessed another act of generosity. Naturally, it, too, involved fish. Two middle-aged guys in a pickup pulled up at the curb—fishermen, judging by their clothes. They got out, and one climbed into the back of the truck and lowered a big cardboard box down to the other guy. He set it on the sidewalk, opened it, and began lifting out huge whole salmon. He gave the wrapped fish to elderly passersby, and to a few others. This continued until the pickup was empty and all the fish handed out. I learned it's a regular event, called the "senior giveaway." Cordova District Fishermen United has been doing it for years. Hundreds of local fishers designate a portion of their catches to give away.

Most of the locals with whom I talked were keenly aware that they lived in the kind of close-knit, close-to-nature community that is an endangered species in 21st-century America. They deeply appreciate this privilege, and they intend to protect it. Many of the pickups in town bear bumper stickers that read "No Road"—a to-the-point statement referring to the ongoing pressure by some business boosters to build a road to connect Cordova to the outside. The majority of locals think this is a terrible idea that likely would lead to runaway growth and diminish the town's unique character.

The boosters accuse the no-roaders of living in the past, but I don't think that's accurate. On the contrary, it seems to me that the boosters are the ones living in the past in the pejorative sense. They're lobbying for the painfully familiar and increasingly discredited mall-and-chain-store blight that already has degraded most of the country, a style of development that makes a few quick bucks for a few people—most of them absentee investors and distant corporate officers—at the cost of a community's soul. The no-roaders don't resist everything modern—they've got the Internet, they've got satellite TV, and you should see the sophisticated electronic gear they've got in their fishing boats. They simply resist what they see as the harmful aspects of modernity.

EARLY ONE MORNING I WITNESSED THE FORESIGHT WITH WHICH CORDOVANS address the future. I walked down to the harbor and boarded the *Summertime Sage*, owned

In Alaganik Slough in the Copper River Delta, a trumpeter swan
vigorously flaps its seven-foot wingspan. Five to seven percent
of the world's trumpeter swans—the largest of all North American waterfowl—
come to the delta every summer to build their nests and hatch their young.

Many cascades tumble through the rain forest around Cordova.

It's not surprising: The area gets nearly 170 inches of rain a year.

and captained by Dan Bilderback. Bilderback has been commercial fishing for decades, but that day we weren't going out on an ordinary fishing trip.

Two other people, Brad Reynolds and Marguerite Leeds, joined us on the ship-shape little vessel. Reynolds is a biologist and Leeds a field tech, both at the Prince William Sound Science Center—a research institution on the north side of the Cordova harbor, not geared to visitors but with a few exhibits and staff happy to answer questions about the sound and the delta. The two scientists and Bilderback set up two framed nets that reminded me of small soccer goals and secured them to moveable arms on the boat, one on each side. At designated points around the delta Bilderback lowered the nets and the researchers took a sampling of the fish, with a particular interest in out-migrating juvenile salmon. They also took salinity, temperature, and other readings. This weekly survey was part of a multiyear study being conducted by the science center. Reynolds said that in Cordova, fishers seem to appreciate scientific information about the condition of their fisheries more than elsewhere; the Cordovans don't want to over-fish the local stocks, as so many others have. They want plenty of fish to be there for their children and grandchildren.

The gray sky hung low and a chilly wind blew across the water as we made our way southwest down Orca Inlet. As we passed a couple of sea otters, Bilderback said that 30 years ago they'd almost vanished from the area, but now they'd rebounded and thousands inhabit the inlet and delta. Sure enough, maybe three minutes later I saw a group of about twenty otters, one lifting its torso out of the water repeatedly, as if doing stomach crunches. Over the next five minutes I saw two dozen more scattered about.

Before our heading could dump us into the perilous waters of the open Gulf of Alaska, we rounded a point and turned southeast through a narrow channel surrounded by mudflats. This was the western edge of the Copper River Delta, the fan-shaped mix of open water, sandbars, mudflats, and wetlands built on the foundation of silt washing down from the coastal and interior mountains via the mighty Copper River. The delta covers 700,000 acres, and at its mouth measures some 50 miles across, making it the largest wetland ecosystem on the Pacific coast of North America.

The delta is a bountiful ecosystem. It's a prolific nursery for fish, but it also is beloved by birds migrating up the Pacific Flyway. Migratory birds use stopovers to refuel before continuing their energy-draining, long-distance flights. A notable three to five million shorebirds come to this delta annually, making it the biggest stopover on the fly-way. Add in the permanent avian residents, and 16 million shorebirds and waterfowl make use of the Copper River Delta each year.

Next-door neighbor to the delta, Cordova is a natural place to host an annual bird-watching event, which they've been doing since 1990. The three-day Copper River Delta Shorebird Festival in May attracts hundreds of visitors, who attend birding work-shops, tank up on pancakes at the Birder's Breakfast at St. Joe's Catholic Church, listen to talks by birding experts, and enjoy the Birder's Bash and Dinner Cruise together.

As the *Summertime Sage* continued across the mouth of the delta, I saw bald eagles here and there, the occasional sea lion or harbor seal, and a nesting island thronged by noisy kittiwakes, pigeon guillemots, and cormorants. But most of all I saw more sea otters, hundreds of them, as many as 80 in a single gathering. Sometimes large groups were hauled out on sandbars, like seals and sea lions: a sight I haven't seen elsewhere. At our approach, a few of the more skittish otters would head for the water, their arched backs and sinuous movements revealing their membership in the weasel family. Bilderback noted that crab fishers wish the otter population weren't quite so prosperous, as otters eat loads of coveted Dungeness crabs.

A couple of hours into the boat trip, the rain stopped and the clouds thinned. Thank goodness, because heavy weather would have prevented my next ride from arriving. We heard the drone of the floatplane well before we saw it. The four-seater touched down a few hundred yards west of the boat, flinging a long rooster tail of white spray in its wake before it slowed down and taxied up to us. Wishing my companions well as they sampled the delta for the rest of the day, I took a long step across to the pontoon and hauled myself into the cockpit. The pilot pushed off from the boat, climbed up after me, shouted over the idling engine, "Hi, I'm Terry Kennedy"—and we were off. Kennedy, his father, and his son were all pilots. He had been flying for 43 years.

We scooted across the water, bouncing more than a bit, until we'd built up enough speed to lift off. Moments later we leveled off at about 500 feet, and I had a bird's-eye view of the delta. Directly below us sprawled a spare, flat, oddly desertlike realm of dark blue water, gray-brown mudflats, and tan sandbars patterned with close-set wavy lines. A group of about 150 hauled-out harbor seals presented another pattern. Awkward on land, harbor seals tend to stay close to the water, so these 150 creatures had lined up sideways, one beside the next, each right by the water's edge along the curving fringe of a sandbar. If I squinted, they looked like the dark feet of a millipede.

Fishing boats formed yet another pattern as they lay at anchor, single file, in some of the larger channels. Kennedy explained that they were waiting for the next "opener": a designated period, often 24 hours, during which an area is open for commercial fishing—another way to preserve the fisheries. The boats below us were the gill-netters that come out in late spring and early summer to catch sockeye and king salmon. During peak season, the boats stay out in the delta, because it's too expensive and time-consuming to chug back to Cordova every evening. Kennedy and other pilots often fly crew members back and forth between town and boats, so they don't go stir-crazy.

After a while we turned inland. Soon the minimalist landscape of the flats gave way to the vivid green of wetlands—hundreds of soggy square miles of grasses, shrubs, and small trees laced with winding channels and dotted with ponds. Here and there we spotted moose, including one cow shepherding a pair of spindly-legged calves across a meadow. We enjoyed the rare opportunity of seeing eagles from above, and once we flew directly over a treetop nest on which an adult eagle was sitting, presumably keeping some eggs warm.

The tall spruce with the nest was the harbinger of the evergreen forest that we began flying over as we neared the inland boundary of the delta and started up into the coastal mountains. Though we climbed a bit, the 2,000- and 3,000-foot peaks loomed

*Eskimos invented the kayak ages ago, but modern Alaskans
have enthusiastically embraced this venerable mode of water transportation.
Many tour companies, including the owners of this colorful cluster of kayaks,
take visitors on guided kayak tours through the sheltered waters of Prince William Sound.*

above us as we banked around their stony flanks, working our way back toward Cordova by traveling up the rivers and through the passes. We flew over a moonscape of giant ice hummocks covered by a thin brown cloak of debris. The shadow of our little plane rippled across a couple of glaciers, including the Sheridan, whose aqua crevasses ran lengthwise instead of the usual crosswise. From the air we also could see ice pools—radiant, dark blue bodies of water lying at the bottom of shallow fissures.

MY DESCRIPTION SO FAR MIGHT SUGGEST THAT THE ONLY WAY TO EXPLORE the delta is by boat or plane, but I've been holding out on you. Travelers can drive out the Copper River Highway, a 50-mile, mostly gravel, dead-end road that cuts through the more terrestrial northern section of the delta. If you don't bring your vehicle on the ferry, there are a couple of local car rental outfits and a wonderful, knowledgeable Cordova woman, Becky Chapek, who runs bus and van tours out the highway.

I got to ride out the road with two guys whose agency helps manage the delta: Forest Service employees Bob Behrends (the guy who danced with the grizzly) and Ken Hodges, a fisheries biologist. We headed east out of town in their government-issue SUV, skirting Eyak Lake and crossing the Eyak River. Around milepost 7—the count starts at the ferry dock—we entered the delta through the Gap, an almost sea-level pass that leads through the mountains that frame Cordova. While the town gets drenched by about 167 inches of precipitation a year, the world east of the Gap receives only about half as much. The landscape changes radically, too, from a mountainous conifer forest to a flat terrain of meadows and wetlands, though the heavily treed mountains hover just a couple of miles to the north, and sometimes bulge in closer. A few decades ago the land just south of the highway was a blend of ponds and knee-high vegetation, but a monster earthquake, magnitude 9.2, shook Prince William Sound in March 1964 and raised much of the delta about six feet, draining off some of the water and allowing alder, willows, and eventually spruce to invade. By creating more dry land, the quake even pushed the ocean shore about half a mile farther south.

As we drove into the delta, admiring the profusion of lupine lining the road and purpling the meadows, I spied a pair of white swans cruising regally in a pond. Trumpeters, said Behrends; five to seven percent of the world's trumpeter swans nest in this delta. We saw many more in the course of the day, though we never heard the call that earned them their name. We also saw the dark heads of dusky Canada geese popping up out of the grassy meadows; almost all of the world's duskies nest here. To the north, Scott and Sheridan Glaciers flashed their icy smiles down at us. At milepost 17 we took a side road to Alaganik Slough, where we strolled a boardwalk. When the hooligan spawn, the slough becomes a riot as eagles, gulls, ravens, and bears crowd in to feed on the fishy multitude.

The landscape shifted again around milepost 27, when we reached the western-most branch of the Copper River. For the next ten miles a series of bridges allowed the

Warmly clothed kayakers paddle amid icebergs that break off

from the glaciers that flow into Prince William Sound.

road to leap from island to island across broad channels of this mammoth outpouring of water. The wind was calm that day, but often it howls out of the interior and blasts down the river at 70 or 80 miles an hour. Behrends and Hodges showed me where the gale-driven sand had gouged holes in the wooden guardrail posts on one of the bridges.

From here the highway turned due north and followed the river to the end of the road at the Million Dollar Bridge. Built across the Copper River in 1910, the bridge enabled trains to carry copper from a rich mine in the interior down to seagoing ships. The bridge got its extravagant name because it cost a great deal—bridging a major river between two active glaciers is no mean feat. After the mine closed in 1938, the railroad and bridge fell into disuse. In the 1940s and 1950s, the highway was built over the old railway and the bridge was converted to carry vehicles. But that use ended abruptly when the 1964 earthquake knocked the fourth span into the river.

Behrends, Hodges, and I parked in the campground beside the bridge and walked a few hundred yards to a small interpretive site at the river's edge. With all its braided streams funneled into a single quarter-mile-wide channel, the Copper River was impressive, as were the icebergs floating past. The far bank stole the show, though, because there towered the roughly 300-foot-high front of Childs Glacier. Like the craggy visage of an old boxer who's lost more bouts than he's won, the glacier's face bore deep, ragged scars, made when great hunks of ice broke off and fell into the river below. Behrends told me about "glacier fishing"—that's when the glacier calves a big enough hunk of ice to produce a wave that sweeps across the river and heaves fish up on the sloping bank below, where people can pick up the writhing future fillets. Grizzly bears, bald eagles, and gulls patrol the bank, too, looking for an easy meal.

Once in a great while these waves turn out to be monsters. In 1993 pretty much the entire face of the glacier belly-flopped into the river and sent out a tsunami that could have tossed a blue whale onto the shore. Three women admiring the glacier from the interpretive site saw the 30- to 40-foot wall of water coming and ran into the woods, but the onrushing wave crossed the river in seconds and washed right over the bank, catching up to the fleeing women and tumbling them head over heels. Happily, they all survived, though two spent some time in the hospital. One of the women told Behrends that when the water finally receded, she came out of her daze to find that an enormous, writhing snake had been deposited right beside her. Screaming, she struggled to her feet and backed away in horror. She didn't back away too far, however, before she sheepishly realized that the writhing creature actually was a big salmon.

To top off our day we drove across the Million Dollar Bridge, which had been repaired and opened to vehicle traffic in 2005. Of course it didn't lead anywhere other than to the construction site on the opposite bank, but that may change in the future. The old railroad grade along the Copper River winds about 70 miles through the coast range to the town of Chitina, which connects by road to the rest of Alaska and the outside world. This is the route on which the Cordova boosters want to build a road. Was it wrong of me to wish for a localized earthquake with its epicenter right under the bridge, one just strong enough to do the job of keeping Cordova Cordova? ■

This male sockeye salmon, native to Alaskan waters, has donned its spawning colors of red and green and is now prepared to fertilize the eggs that female sockeye will deposit in the gravel. Millions of salmon return each year to the Copper River and its tributaries to spawn, perpetuating one of North America's most celebrated fisheries.

A melting iceberg drifting through Prince William Sound

catches the first rays of the rising sun.

Where the wild things are

Cordova and the Copper River Delta are known for their
salmon, but the area also offers much to visitors whose
definition of wildlife is not limited to an animal served on
a platter with a wedge of lemon. Moose, river otters,
bald eagles, mountain goats: A diverse assemblage of
wildlife inhabits this varying landscape of near-shore ocean,
tidal flats, wetlands, rivers, and upland forests.

Both grizzly bears and black bears roam the Copper River Delta, so hikers should be on the alert, not only for safety's sake, but for the sheer thrill of sighting them. A commonly uttered rule of thumb is to stay at least one hundred yards away from a bear. The group opposite got closer than that—but only because they had hiked to an official bear-viewing area with a knowledgeable guide.

If you're not lucky enough to spot a bear—at a safe distance—perhaps you'll at least see signs, freshly left in the mud, such as the unmistakable lumbering line of bear tracks on page 68.

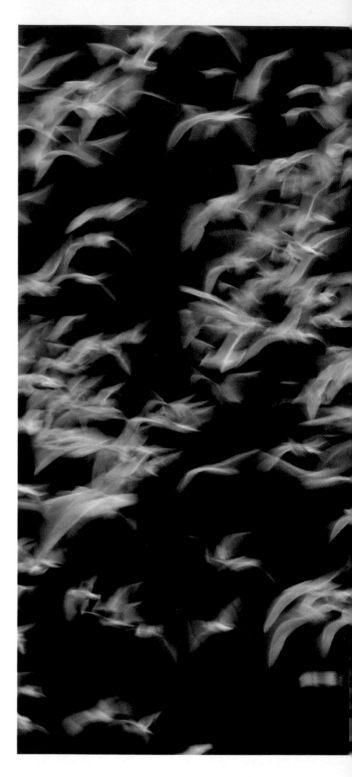

Shorebirds by the millions migrate through the Copper River Delta every spring and fall. Least sandpipers, black-bellied plovers, greater yellowlegs, ruddy turnstones, whimbrels, and about 20 other shorebird species stop in this rich delta to feed and rest. On a given day in late April to mid-May, visitors can travel a few miles south of Cordova to Hartney Bay and see maybe 40,000 or 50,000 shorebirds stilting around the mudflats, with seabirds like the gulls at right flashing in close formation.

The waters bordering the mudflats shelter their own array of animals, including killer whales, harbor seals, sea lions, and sea otters, below. During the 18th- and 19th-century European exploration—and exploitation—of Alaska, traders sought valuable pelts. They drove the sea otter to the brink of extinction, but the species rebounded. Today, thousands swim near Cordova and the delta.

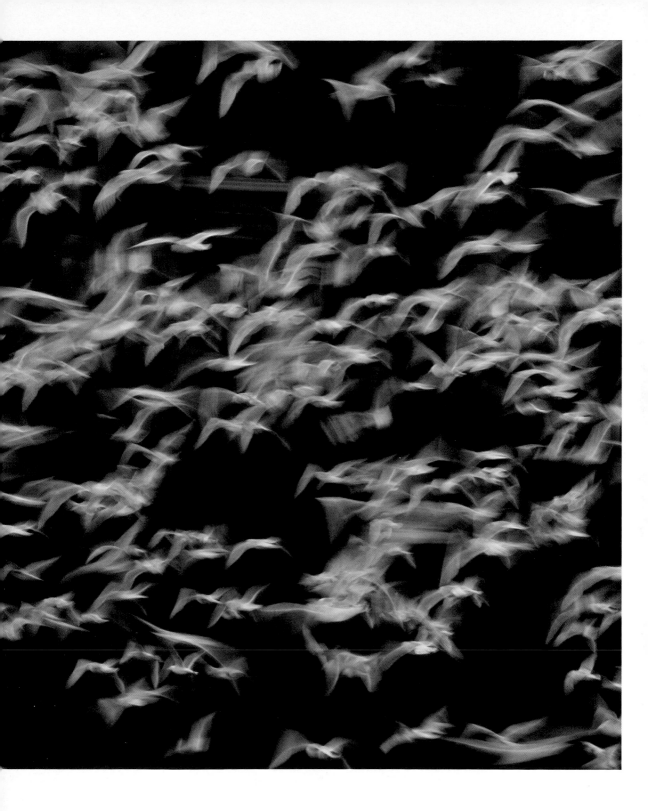

CHAPTER THREE

Across the waters of
KACHEMAK BAY

Float planes provide access to the remote locales of Kachemak Bay, both civilized and wild.

Homer Spit extends several miles into the waters of Kachemak Bay, a western reach of Alaska's Kenai Peninsula.

ACROSS THE WATERS OF KACHEMAK BAY

The Southern Kenai Peninsula

D ON'T LET HOMER SEDUCE YOU. I'VE FELT THE SIREN CALL SEVERAL TIMES myself, and I know how enticing it can be.

Recently I once again drove the 220 miles southwest from Anchorage, winding across the beautiful Kenai Peninsula and then following the Sterling Highway south along Cook Inlet. I stopped at the overlook above Homer and looked down on the storied town at the end of the road and the tip of the peninsula. To the south I saw Kachemak Bay and, on its far side, the glaciers and ever snowbound peaks of the Kenai Mountains. To the west I saw the Pacific Ocean in the form of Cook Inlet and the roughly 4,000 feet of the Augustine Volcano that rise above the inlet's waters as Augustine Island, and the jagged mountains 70 miles away on the far side of the inlet. Irresistible…

I drove on down into Homer and spent a few days there. Sure, I was intrigued by the Alaska Islands and Ocean Center, a new museum/visitor center/research institute that dazzles with its state-of-the-art interactive exhibits. And I savored the organic lemon-peppered halibut salad and the puffin muffins at Fresh Sourdough Express, one of several notable eateries that you would never expect to find in a road's-end Alaskan town of 4,000 people. Nor can I deny that I enjoyed the many art galleries, which feature the work of the droves of local artists, some with statewide or even national reputations.

I got a particular kick out of the found-item sculptures of Don Henry, such as the eagle he fashioned from old kitchen utensils, somehow both goofy and beautiful. Henry scrounges most of his materials from yard sales and the like, but a gallery employee told me that on occasion Henry finds his utensils at home, resulting in dismayed shouts from his wife when she starts preparing for a dinner party and discovers that all the forks are gone.

Yes, Homer is charming. But if you let that charm seduce you, then you'll never explore the glorious world beyond, across the waters of Kachemak Bay and Cook Inlet. On my two previous visits I'd failed to extricate myself from Homer's embrace and had never crossed the bay or the inlet, but this time I made it. Turns out, the world across the water is powerfully seductive in its own right.

THE LIGHT RAIN DAMPENED OUR CLOTHING BUT NOT OUR ENTHUSIASM AS half a dozen fellow travelers and I boarded the boat in the Homer harbor. Led by our guide, Marilyn Sigman, the executive director of the Center for Alaskan Coastal Studies, we were heading out for an all-day natural history tour of Kachemak Bay and the land across the bay. The center runs these trips daily during the summer, providing an opportunity not only to relish the scenery but to learn about the intricacies beneath the surface of this picture-postcard setting. Visitors can learn about daily center events by stopping at the Yurt on the Spit—a portable Mongolian hut that stands on the spit in Homer's harbor, houses a gift shop, and serves as the tour departure point as well.

As soon as we left the harbor and the protection of the breakwater, the wind-driven swells began rocking our boat. Nothing drastic, but let's just say that trying to keep binoculars trained on a passing sea otter proved fruitless. So as the boat churned south across the bay, we huddled under the roofed part of the deck, out of the rain, and Sigman told us a bit about the remarkable body of water beneath us.

Kachemak Bay cuts about 30 miles into the Kenai Peninsula and measures some five to ten miles across. It is an estuary, where fresh water from melting glaciers in the summer mixes with the nutrient-rich seawater to create a highly productive ecosystem. At the top of this lavish food chain are animals like beluga whales, bald eagles, sea otters, harbor seals, the thousands of shorebirds that feast in the marshes at the head of the bay, and the 200-pound halibut that anglers chase on charter boats out of Homer. (Homer's nickname is the "Halibut Fishing Capital of the World.") Due to the bay's importance and outstanding qualities, it is one of 25 estuaries in the National Estuarine Research Reserve System.

After about 20 minutes we neared Gull Island, a rocky outcropping just a few hundred yards from the southern shore. As the name promises, gulls favor this small island, as do black-legged kittiwakes, pigeon guillemots, common murres, tufted puffins, horned puffins, pelagic cormorants, and red-faced cormorants. All these species seek out this place to nest, protected from terrestrial predators by the saltwater moat.

During the summer about 16,000 birds occupy Gull Island. Normally we'd have tarried, slowly motoring along the perimeter of the island, but the wind had picked up and the sea had grown so choppy that we had to scoot by the island and get to shore.

The Center for Alaskan Coastal Studies maintains a field station on the mainland at the mouth of Peterson Bay, less than a mile from Gull Island. Our group disembarked on a floating wooden platform about 50 yards offshore and used a rope-and-pulley system to haul the platform and ourselves to the stairs at the bottom of the seaside bluff. At the top we beheld the handsome, two-story log exterior of the station's main building, set amid old-growth coastal forest. We trooped up onto the generous deck that encircles the main building, where Sigman directed us to a pair of "live tanks." They looked like five-by-five-foot tables until we lifted off the wooden lids to reveal shallow saltwater habitats inside them, teeming with intertidal creatures.

I saw a decorator crab spidering across the bottom on its long, spindly legs; its name comes from its habit of gluing bits of seaweed to its shell for camouflage. A sculpin—an explosively quick, finger-length fish—flashed through the water and found refuge under a rock overhang. Sigman invited us to stroke the raspy, leathery back of a gumboot chiton; at nearly a foot in length, it's the largest chiton species in the world. Gumboot chitons resemble half a football that's been cut lengthwise, and they attach to rocks with muscular feet, scraping off algae to eat with a tonguelike appendage.

Hermit crabs of several varieties, including one brilliant orange fellow, hunkered in their stolen shells. As hermit crabs grow, they move into bigger and bigger abandoned shells. Knowing this, some of the field station's staffers—remember, this is a remote facility with little conventional entertainment—occasionally amuse themselves by placing a bunch of hermit crabs together in a small space, then dropping in a big come-hither shell and watching them fight over it.

Arguably, the most fascinating creatures in the tanks were the sea stars, aka starfish, although they're not fish at all. About a dozen species inhabited the tank. I saw my first morning sunstar, a species that grows to be about a foot and a half in diameter, sports 8 to 15 rays (or legs), and comes in orange, brown, or yellow. This one was demonstrating typical sea star feeding behavior: It had used its hydraulically operated tube feet to pry open a mussel, just wide enough to allow it to insert its own stomach through the crack between the two halves of the mussel shell. Now the sea star's stomach was digesting the mussel's body inside the mussel's own shell. There's a horror movie waiting to be made.

At the top of the sea star firmament is the sunflower star, the tiger of the tide pool. Though the one we saw was a mere youth that measured only 10 or 12 inches across, sunflower stars are among the world's largest sea stars, reaching diameters of 40 inches. They're also the world's fastest sea stars; when sprinting, they can cover ten feet a minute. When sunflower stars show up, snails, limpets, and other mobile

Truly a town that looks to the water, Homer, Alaska, includes a harbor that

houses hundreds of commercial fishing and recreational vessels.

prey scatter—if an animal can be said to "scatter" when it moves literally slower than molasses. I saw a panicked sea urchin—one of those red-purple pincushiony critters—trying to race away from an approaching sunflower star, but it was no contest. Within half a minute the star had overtaken the terrified urchin. However, for whatever reason, the sunflower star passed by the sea urchin, which proceeded to a corner—I imagined it trembling and panting. It was still there, cowering, 20 minutes later when we left the station.

From the station we hiked into the surrounding spruce forest, making our way south on a network of trails. Sigman showed us the pink-purple blossoms of salmonberry, the white umbels of elderberry, and the little pink blooms of currant. She pointed out various lichens, including the endearingly named fairy puke lichen, and she discussed the cycle of decay and rebirth in the forest. When we came across a false azalea, she informed us that it emits a scent that discourages mosquitoes, so locals often tuck sprigs of this natural repellent behind their ears, which she proceeded to do. The mozzies weren't bad that day, but they weren't gone on holiday, either, so I followed Sigman's lead.

After an hour or so we emerged from the forest onto a rocky beach on the north shore of China Poot Bay. This small bay is very shallow, and we arrived at low tide, so most of the water had drained out, exposing mudflats and a sizeable expanse of rocky bottom. That was precisely why Sigman had brought us here at this time. Instead of poking around in the tanks on the deck of the field station, we were going to explore wild tide pools and intertidal habitat.

As we crunched along the cobble-and-gravel beach, buried clams sent up spouts of water, sometimes geysering as high as four or five feet. We stopped at some larger rocks, and Sigman noted the barnacles cemented to the surface; she said that the glue they use is so strong and works so well under wet conditions that researchers are trying to adapt it for use in dentistry. We passed a tide pool in which we spied a yellow mass of snail eggs and a red ribbon worm, a bloodred creature that can reach lengths of six feet.

I gently lifted a small rock and found a three-inch-long silky sea cucumber, pink and tan and translucent. We saw veritable herds of sea stars working the mussel beds. Stopping at another big rock, Sigman pointed at a pile of clam shells and sea urchin skeletons on the ground in front of a little cave that went under the rock. An octopus den, she said. Not only could she tell by the evidence of its feasts, but she had also seen this particular giant Pacific octopus before, though we didn't spot it that day. Octopuses of this species come by the adjective in their name honestly, as they can weigh up to one hundred pounds and boast tentacles that can stretch 30 feet long.

After an hour or two of rummaging among the tide pools, we hiked back to the field station, and I said goodbye to Sigman and some of the others in the tour group. For me and two other folks, though, the tour wasn't over. We'd signed on for the kayak option, so we went back down to the floating dock and met up with two

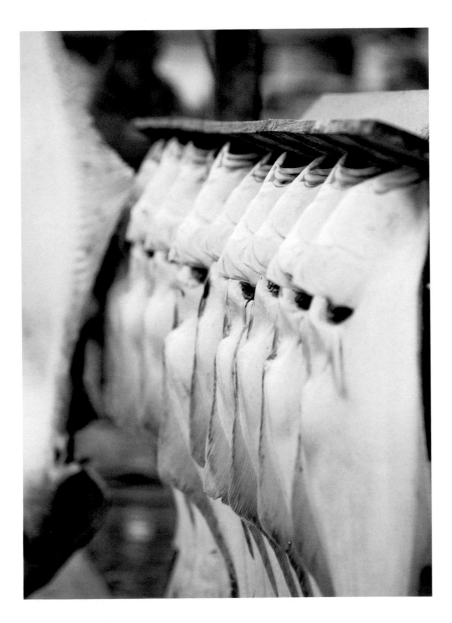

This dockside rack of hanging halibut demonstrates the credibility of Homer's claim to be the "Halibut Fishing Capital of the World." Though most anglers lust for "barn door" halibut—the monsters that weigh 200, 300, and even 400 pounds—smaller halibut make better eating.

Every summer thousands of gulls, cormorants, puffins, and kittiwakes

make their nests on Gull Island, in Kachemak Bay.

other kayakers and Don Williamson, the bearded veteran of the world's oceans who was our guide. For the first 30 minutes, Williamson was more instructor than guide. Travelers with little or no kayak experience often decide to go on these outings, and Williamson wanted to make sure even the greenest paddler would be safe and comfortable.

Once he had confirmed that everyone was shipshape, we headed out the west side of Peterson Bay into the more open waters of Kachemak Bay. The weather had improved markedly since the morning's bumpy crossing, and the water had grown reasonably smooth. We struck out toward Gull Island, about half a mile distant. I'd barely settled into the push-pull rhythm of paddling when we spotted a gray whale spouting a few hundred yards to the west. It soon went around a point of land, however, so we surrendered any thoughts of giving chase and continued toward the bird colony, our destination.

LONG BEFORE WE REACHED THE ISLAND WE BEGAN SEEING SEABIRDS on the water or flying overhead. First we saw a solitary tufted puffin: stocky black body the size of a small duck, white face, massive yellow-and-orange bill, and the two eponymous, three-inch tufts of cream-colored feathers trailing back from its eyes. Mostly, though, we kayaked past common murres, hundreds and thousands of them in tight formations, bobbing on the swells. As we drew within 50 yards of the rocks, we entered the avian vortex, the whirlwind of incessantly screaming gulls and kittiwakes flying in circles around the island. Beneath this crowd our waterproof rain gear did double duty.

When we got within about ten yards of the island, we began slowly circling it ourselves, sometimes drifting quietly for several minutes before moving on. It seemed that every nook, cranny, ledge, and flat spot was occupied by a seabird, a nest, or both. These critters believed in compact development, not sprawl. A few were still adding to their nests, flying in carrying sticks or grass. Some pairs acted like smitten lovers, rubbing bills and giving each other tender nibbles.

In contrast, I saw two gulls engaged in a bloody fight that went well beyond the usual harmless squabbling. Amazingly, given all the activity and commotion, a number of birds were asleep. On top of the highest rock a couple of bald eagles perched on the bare branches of a small dead tree. Not there to nest, these interlopers were on the prowl for some easy pickings. They seemed to make the other birds nervous.

After about an hour with the birds, we headed back toward the shore. The sun had emerged to brighten the blue of the bay. To the northeast a rainbow shone brilliantly against the backdrop of retreating dark clouds. Long Beach, one of the bay's few sandy shores, stretched out in front of us, fringed by a grassy meadow and spruce trees. Behind it jutted the glacier-streaked peaks of the Kenai Mountains. Not a bad place to paddle around in a kayak. I was sorry we had to return to the dock, but I was heartened by the knowledge that I'd be back on the bay the next day.

✿

SURE ENOUGH, THE NEXT MORNING I WAS ONCE AGAIN ON KACHEMAK BAY, though this time I wasn't paddling a kayak. I was riding in what Alaskans call a water taxi, in this case a 28-foot aluminum-hulled landing craft.

Most people associate landing craft with the D-Day invasion of World War II, when these flat-hulled boats delivered Allied soldiers onto French beaches. Landing craft work well in the less-developed parts of Alaska—which is almost everywhere—because they don't require docks. Those flat, tough hulls enable them to run up onto beaches or gravel bars to drop off their passengers and freight. During the summer, water taxis based in Homer are busy taking hikers, hunters, kayakers, and anglers across the bay. (Or, as one water taxi operator told me he had done recently, making an emergency delivery of a five-gallon tub of ice cream to a customer with cravings and the money to indulge them.) The passengers either set up a pickup time or call when they're ready to return to Homer.

The captain steered the boat from the small cabin near the back of the landing craft, while an avid amateur photographer named Len and I stood in front on the open deck, hanging onto metal stanchions for support. Neither Len nor I had a strict itinerary. We just wanted to poke along the coastline on the far shore of the bay to see what we could see.

From the Homer harbor we proceeded across the bay to a site called Sixty-Foot Rock, a straightforwardly named island about a mile off the south shore. A smaller version of Gull Island, Sixty-Foot Rock hosts a mob of nesting seabirds during the summer, but that was only our secondary reason for going there. Len was keen to put his huge telephoto lens to work on some sea otters, and our captain knew that a male-female pair often hung out around the rock. And there they were, their round, whiskered faces peering up at us from a kelp bed about 20 yards away. Len clicked away and I watched as the otters daintily groomed each other and then climbed up onto a ledge near the bottom of the rock.

From Sixty-Foot Rock we chugged northeast along the coast, passing the mouth of now-familiar China Poot Bay, lingering at Gull Island (which I was perfectly happy to visit again), and rounding Peterson Point on our way to the community of Halibut Cove, six miles southeast of Homer.

In the early 1900s, this town was the hub of a prosperous herring fishery, home to about a thousand people and dozens of salteries. The fishery went bust in 1928 and the place nearly became a ghost town, but a few decades ago people started trickling back in, reincarnating Halibut Cove as a combination artists' hideaway and

Ocher sea stars are one of many species that inhabit the rocky intertidal areas of
Kachemak Bay and other offshoots of Cook Inlet. When the tide is out, tide pool explorers
may find sea anemones, octopuses, gumboot chitons, sea urchins, kelp crabs, and sculpins.
Several other species of sea star also live here, including the spectacular sunflower stars,
which measure as much as three feet in diameter.

fishing village. The 2000 census listed its population at 35, but a more current website counts only 22.

The captain slowed our landing craft to maybe five miles per hour and slipped into town through the narrows between the mainland and Ismailof Island. Yes, you can take a boat right into town, because the lagoonlike body of water between the mainland and the island is the core of Halibut Cove, with buildings along both shorelines and on little islands in the lagoon. There are no roads. The handful of houses (some modest, some swanky), together with the town's galleries, small lodges, the boat-building shop, and one restaurant are all linked by a raised boardwalk. Residents going to visit one another shoot across the lagoon in skiffs or kayaks as often as they walk.

Some of the local artists are highly regarded, notably Diana Tillion, who paints using a medium that includes ink she extracts from octopuses with a hypodermic needle. Arguably the most eccentric cove artist is Alex Combs, who leaves his studio open when he's not there so visitors can look at his work. He puts out a sign asking people who want to buy a painting to take whatever they like and leave behind however much money they consider fair.

I'M REMINDED OF WHAT HAPPENED NEXT BY THE RAGGED LINE THAT RUNS ACROSS page 14 of the notebook in which I was writing as we motored through Halibut Cove. We were just passing the Saltry Restaurant, reputed to offer some of the finest fare in the state. A classic wooden boat brings customers from Homer to the Saltry for lunches and dinners during the summer. My notes read "Supposed to be great restaurant. Long stairs to floating dock of ..."—and then comes that ragged line where my pen raked across the page when our landing craft hit the rock.

You wouldn't think that hitting a submerged rock would have much impact when you're going only five miles per hour, but the result was quite dramatic. I was standing on the deck, using both hands to write in my notebook, so when the boat abruptly stopped, my untethered body rocketed forward. Len later told me that I was almost horizontal when I flew by him on my way to crashing onto the deck, which I skidded across on my hands and knees. Fortunately, I came away with nothing more than scrapes and bruises. Unfortunately, though, Len kept his grip on the stanchion and remained on his feet, making him the one who got more seriously hurt, by smacking his head against the unforgiving stanchion.

As the boat sat there, its front end atop the rock, the captain rushed from the cabin to see if we were all right. I slowly got to my feet and reported that I was in one piece. Len, too, said he was fine, but to the captain and me he looked a bit dazed, so we convinced him to sit down. Right before our eyes, the yellow and purple silver dollar-size bruise on his forehead began to swell into a protruding knot, scary enough to make

A grizzly wades through the shallows in Katmai National Park and Preserve,

across Cook Inlet and south from the Kenai on the Alaska Peninsula.

us check his pupils to see if one was dilated more than the other, an indication of a concussion. His pupils looked normal, thank goodness, but we decided he needed ice for his head and a place to lie down for a while. The captain backed us off the rock and docked at the Saltry.

By the time we helped Len to the top of the long stairway, he said that his head was starting to throb. He lay down on a bench on the restaurant's deck under the watchful eye of the captain while I went in search of ice. Inside, I encountered Marian Beck, co-owner of the restaurant, who quickly filled a plastic bag with ice and brought it to Len.

Letting Len rest awhile, we all sat around, talking together. Beck told us that Halibut Cove residents referred to the rock on which we'd run aground as Speed Bump Rock. It wasn't on most charts, and people who didn't live around there ran into it all the time, especially when the tide was in, just high enough to cover it but not high enough to let boats pass safely over it. I told her about my brief flight. She said that was nothing—she remembered someone who'd smashed into the rock and launched a passenger all the way across the bow and out of the boat. Beck laughed and said her husband even hit the rock once, despite having lived with it for years.

Once Len was safely on ice and we'd settled down a bit, the captain began apologizing. He continued apologizing on and off until we parted ways about an hour later. First and foremost he worried about Len, but in addition he was ashamed, humiliated even. He kept saying that running aground is the worst thing a captain can do. He said he'd been driving boats for more than 30 years and had never hit a rock before. Clearly he was a veteran sea salt and a responsible guy. It seemed to me that under the circumstances, anyone could have hit Speed Bump Rock, so I decided to save him further embarrassment by not using his name in this book. He'll just have to go down in history as "the captain."

After resting and communing with the bag of ice for half an hour, Len seemed better, but Captain Anonymous and I thought he still should get his head examined. So we cut short our coastal ramblings. The captain dropped me off just around the corner at my next stop, Peterson Bay Lodge, and then hightailed it back to Homer. I hoped Len would be fine.

On a floating dock about a hundred yards from the head of Peterson Bay, I met one of my hosts for the next 24 hours, Gary Seims, who owns and runs the lodge along with his wife, Debbie. Theirs is one of about a half a dozen backcountry lodges that dot the south coast of Kachemak Bay—personal, intimate operations that cater to only 5 to 15 guests at a time. These establishments range from rustic-ritzy to basic, and the Seimses' place fell about in the middle of the luxury scale. Backcountry lodges are a great alternative for travelers who want to spend time in the Alaskan wilds but are unable or unwilling to deal with backpacking and tenting.

When I arrived, Gary was standing at a table sorting oysters. That's the Seimses' other business. He and Debbie were among those who pioneered oyster farming in the cold, clean waters of Kachemak Bay in the early 1990s. In 2005, Gary was serving as president of the 13-member oyster co-op, which was doing well as the demand for the Kachemak Bay brand of oysters kept increasing.

An hour later, I learned why demand was growing. Debbie had come out in a skiff to take us ashore, and we'd trooped up to the expansive deck of the main house, where Gary, Debbie, and their son, Tux, live. I loitered by the fire on the deck for a while, watching the sea otters paddle about in the bay, until it was time for the nightly ritual of the oyster hour. Several other guests and I bellied up to the bar, and one of the staff served us oyster after oyster after oyster. I'm generally lukewarm about raw oysters, but I couldn't get enough of these fat, fresh beauties. Well, that's not literally true: I did get enough, because they gave me as many as I wanted, which was about half a dozen. I also munched about half a dozen cooked oysters, which were equally scrumptious.

While we were slurping oysters, Gary and Debbie answered our questions about their life at the edge of civilization. They'd built the house with their own hands, mostly using lumber from trees that they'd logged themselves on the property. For years, every weekday, Gary and Debbie had taken Tux across the bay to school in Homer and back again. A former full-time commercial fisherman, Gary still takes off every July to net sockeye salmon in Cook Inlet with his son and brother.

After dinner, still with plenty of light, Gary, his black Lab (named Popo), and I hiked uphill through the spruce forest and over a ridge to a viewpoint hundreds of feet above a beautiful bay, hemmed in by forest and mountains. Gary said he often spots black bears on the far shore. There's also a creek down there where he takes guests to dip net for sockeye. A trail winds down from the viewpoint to the bay and along its north shore into Kachemak Bay State Park, the 380,000-acre preserve that encompasses much of this land across Kachemak Bay. Tempting—but it was getting late, so we headed back.

On a knoll above the main house is a guest lodge, which houses a kitchen, a sitting room with views of Peterson Bay, an outdoor deck, a barbeque and fire pit, showers, and a sauna. This is a communal facility, used by all the guests. Sleeping quarters consist of several tent-cabins scattered about the hillside. They're screened in to protect against mosquitoes, and guests can close a heavy canvas flap for privacy. But I left the flap in my tent-cabin open so I could see Peterson Bay and environs as I lay in bed. I fell asleep wondering what it would be like to live here, and to live so close to the land, as the Seimses did. I decided I wouldn't want to do it permanently, but I sure was enjoying it at the moment.

THERE'S BEAR-WATCHING, AND THEN THERE'S BEAR-WATCHING, IF YOU KNOW what I mean.

You don't know what I mean?

Well, neither did I when I signed up to go see the bears at Hallo Bay.

Bear-watching is a popular activity at several sites along the coast in southeast and south-central Alaska. I'm not talking about the random spotting of a grizzly or black bear in a national park, but organized viewing opportunities that bring guided groups of visitors to a certain place at a certain time when bears are sure to be there. Most of the time the whereabouts of bears is unpredictable, but the exception is when they gather to feast on salmon, because salmon are predictable. Salmon return from the ocean to spawn in the streams in which they were born, and they make this final journey of their lives on a timetable almost punctual enough to satisfy a train conductor. The bears know when and where the salmon will be, so people know when and where the bears will be.

Over the last few decades, a number of bear hot spots along rivers and creeks on public lands have been developed for bear-watching. Typically there's a platform or some kind of designated spot above the river or creek from which a small group of visitors views the bears. A park ranger, a licensed tour operator, or some other official guide takes the people to that spot and stays there with them. For the safety of the people and the bears, visitors are briefed about proper behavior around bears—and most guides carry a rifle or shotgun, though situations that require the use of a weapon are exceedingly rare. The bears are focused on the salmon, and they're used to that little cluster of people up there in that spot above the river. Meanwhile, the visitors know not to bring smoked salmon sandwiches for lunch, etc. It's a safe system. I asked around and didn't hear of any case in which a person at one of these designated viewing spots had been mauled or killed by a bear.

However—though I didn't know it when I started out—the folks at Hallo Bay don't use this system of bear watching. They have a different approach.

Hallo Bay is a small notch on the eastern shore of the Alaska Peninsula, 120 air miles southwest across Cook Inlet from Homer. It is part of Katmai National Park and Preserve, but it is utterly separate from the developed part of the park dozens of miles to the west. Starting in the late 1980s, a nature lover named Clint Hlebechuk has developed a small, unobtrusive, eco-friendly wilderness camp, also called Hallo Bay, on his 2.5-acre private inholding just north of the bay itself.

That's where four other would-be bear watchers and I were heading when we took off from the Homer airport one overcast June morning. Though travelers often spend several days at Hallo Bay, we'd signed up for the quickie: a five-hour tour. The pilot, Mike Hughes, took us over Kachemak Bay—just as spectacular from the air as from the land or water—and then steered the six-seater on a diagonal course across Cook Inlet.

Soon the clouds closed in and the views diminished, but about 30 minutes later, as we were nearing the far shore, the sky opened up and revealed Cook Inlet and the Alaska Peninsula in all their considerable glory. We saw Augustine Volcano, the poorly named Barren Islands, and then the mainland jumble of rocky coast, sandy beaches, grassy tidal meadows, conifer forest, milky-green glacier-fed rivers, the glaciers that feed them, and the mountains from which the rivers of ice flow.

A grizzly makes its way beneath the Trans-Alaska Pipeline, which runs 800 miles from Arctic oil fields to the port at Valdez, in southern Alaska. The bears of Hallo Bay enjoy a pristine environment, but elsewhere Alaskan wildlife has to contend with industrial growth, especially oil and gas development.

Flying along the coast at about 500 feet, we also caught a first glimpse of our quarry—the renowned Alaskan brown bear. Brown bears are much like their fellow subspecies, the grizzlies, but they live in the coastal areas of the state and are much larger than their interior cousins. Males can exceed one thousand pounds, largely because of the salmon-rich diet these brownies enjoy.

Hughes set us down on the narrow, not-quite-flat, sandy beach in front of the Hallo Bay camp. Our takeoff from Homer had been delayed a couple of hours by the weather, so the Hallo Bay folks were ready and waiting. As we were getting our gear out of the plane, our guide, John Pendergraft, showed up to greet us. He let us know that, whenever we were ready, it was bear time.

Pendergraft consulted with Hughes, and they decided to bundle us back into the plane for a two-mile hop to a big tidal meadow they call the Keyhole. The salmon weren't running yet, so the bears were more scattered, but Pendergraft thought we'd find some down there. After another beach landing, we got out, watched Hughes take off, and gathered around Pendergraft at the base of the grassy dune that separated the beach from the Keyhole. I noticed he was not carrying a rifle or a shotgun.

This is when I found out about Hallo Bay's approach to bear-watching. I figured Pendergraft would lead us to the platform or such, but instead he explained that we would walk out onto the tidal meadow among the bears. Say what? I've been around bears quite a bit. I've talked to many rangers, wildlife biologists, and hunters about bear safety. Once I even spent a couple of weeks in the wilderness with bear researchers. Never have I heard anyone suggest intentionally walking among bears, especially brown bears. On the contrary, everyone in my experience has suggested staying away from them.

Pendergraft knew all about standard bear safety procedures, of course, but he said that for a variety of reasons the situation around Hallo Bay was different. For example, these bears hadn't been hunted, and they didn't see humans as enemies. The utter remoteness of Hallo Bay meant that these bears had never got hold of backpacks or coolers and therefore had never developed a taste for human food. Also, first Hlebechuk and then other people from the camp had been hanging around these bears for many years, and the bears had grown accustomed to their presence.

Furthermore, continued Pendergraft, the guides were experts in bruin behavior. They often could tell what bears were thinking, and they could sense what they were going to do. Guides even communicate with the bears; Pendergraft taught us the basics of such communication. You skeptics out there should note that Hallo Bay has a perfect safety record, and that only four times in more than a dozen years have bears pressed guides to the point that they pulled out the bear flares that they carry, planning to use them only as a last resort.

Pendergraft finished the briefing by reminding us to obey any instructions he gave us immediately. Then over the top of the dune we went.

IN THE EARLY SUMMER, BEFORE THE SALMON CRANK UP, BROWN BEARS OFTEN DIG for clams on mudflats or graze on the grass in the adjacent tidal meadows. From atop the dune we scanned the mile-diameter Keyhole. We counted five bears either digging or grazing, though all were at least half a mile away. The four other guests and I thought this was excellent—I'd never seen that many brown bears in one place before—but Pendergraft wanted to get us a closer look.

You don't walk straight at bears, though, he said, because they may take your doing that as a sign of aggression. So he watched for a while and tried to figure out where some of the bears were headed. Deciding that a female bear being followed by an amorous male were trending toward the north end of the Keyhole, Pendergraft led us that way in hopes of beating the bears to the spot so we could let them come to us. We tramped through the squelching mud, crossed half-foot-deep channels, and slopped through sodden meadows. Along the way we saw hundreds of enormous brownie tracks.

As we neared the north end, we spied a sizeable boar (male bear) about 200 yards away, sleeping on a low hill just above our destination. Pendergraft watched him carefully. When he stirred and spotted us, Pendergraft immediately instructed us to avert our eyes, a sign of submission. When the bear kept staring, Pendergraft had us try various submissive postures, such as turning our backs, showing our profiles, and, finally, dropping to one knee. But the bear continued watching, so Pendergraft told us we had to back off a bit. We obeyed and moved about 100 yards. That seemed to ease the bear's anxiety; he lay down and went to sleep again.

We didn't really need proof, but this episode showed us all why it was important to listen to our guide. Guests generally do listen, but not always.

One time another guide, Kevin Copley, was walking down the beach near camp with a visiting couple when a big boar surprised them. Copley told them to stay calm and stay put, but when he turned to see how the husband was doing—he'd been trailing slightly—he saw the guy sprinting away down the beach. Copley shouted for him to stop because running sometimes triggers a charge, but the terrified man just kept going. Fortunately, the bear didn't give chase and soon wandered off. Copley went to find the guy and finally discovered him crouching in some willows a full mile down the beach. The guy didn't escape without any consequences, however. That night the whole camp could hear his wife lambasting him for running off and leaving her to face the bear.

At Pendergraft's direction, we sat down on a driftwood log and waited. A female being shadowed by a suitor came within about 150 yards, but then she veered up onto the hill. The boar dutifully followed, and soon they both moved out of sight. Minutes later two young males—probably a mere 400 or 500 pounds each—showed up at the edge of the wooded ridgeline and began playing. Standing on their hind legs

A kayaker paddles through the wide-open spaces of

Kachemak Bay, a popular spot for guided kayak tours.

and tussling like a couple of Greco-Roman wrestlers, they smashed about amid the trees, knocking around 30-foot alders and birches as if they were saplings.

But after 20 minutes they vanished, and the only bears within a quarter mile, other than the snoozing boar on the hill, were two young sows grazing their way along the margin of a meadow. We watched them for a while. Pendergraft decided they were heading our way. He took us to the same margin of that same meadow at a point about 300 yards from the two bears, then led us to a spot about 40 feet back from the meadow's edge. We waited. Sure enough, the feeding bears continued following the curving margin of the meadow, coming closer and closer to us as they grazed on the grass like cows—cows with switchblade claws and dripping fangs.

Exhilaration. Apprehension. Awe. All sorts of feelings tugged at my psyche as the bears came within 100 yards, then 50 yards, then 30 yards. The blonder of the two—sows often have surprisingly light hair—eyed us now and then, and Pendergraft said we'd have to watch her carefully. At that point I wrote in my notebook, "Will this be one of those ironies where I'm writing about the bears and then my writing stops because I just got mauled and all they find is my notebook?"

As they got within 20 yards, Pendergraft told us to avoid sudden movements, loud sounds, or even undoing a zipper. No problem. Personally I wasn't planning even to blink. The bears got so close we could hear every squishy step they took. We could hear the sound of their molars grinding the grass. The two sows slowed, then stopped to graze on a particularly lush stand of grass, not more than 10 yards away from us.

Minutes passed as they worked on that mother lode. The alarms gonging in my head subsided enough for me to admire the bears' luxurious winter coats, which they'd soon shed as they donned their scruffy summer pelts. I watched the bulging muscles rippling beneath the skin on their massive shoulders. I tried to see which teeth they used to clip off the grass. Increasingly, I grew comfortable with being so close to these predators.

Then the blonde bear gave me a jolt. I'd focused my binoculars on her face, which filled the view from 30 feet away, and I was noting the details of her snout and ears and eyes. Suddenly she turned, looked straight at me, and took a step in my direction. A hundred volts crackled down my spine, and adrenalin surged through my system.

A heartbeat later—assuming my heart was still beating—the blonde bear turned away and resumed feeding. But for that long second I'd felt like prey. In that primal moment I'd been carried back thousands of years, to a time when humans lived closer to the beasts of the world, knowing, respecting, and sometimes fearing them.

In that one tick of the clock I'd traveled to a place that no boat or plane could ever take me. ■

Framed by mountains and the rich, cold waters of Kachemak Bay and Cook Inlet, Homer ranks as one of the most comely towns in Alaska. Its location also makes it the perfect jumping-off point for travelers who want to explore the remote lands that lie beyond those bodies of water.

Hulking mountains squeeze the shores of Kenai Lake,

a slender body of water on the Kenai Peninsula.

Wilderness outposts

Many Alaskans still live close to the land

to some degree, from full-time subsistence hunters

and fishers who reside in the bush

to those who do some weekend camping

and pack away a few salmon in the freezer.

Visitors can sample this premodern life

in a variety of ways on the Kenai Peninsula.

If you want to wake up to the sounds of nature and not the roar of traffic, the area across Kachemak Bay from Homer is ideal. You can reach this raw land of mountains, glaciers, forests, and coves only by boat or small plane. Experienced backpackers can venture into the unspoiled depths of Kachemak Bay State Park and set up their tents far from the madding crowd.

But, you might question, isn't remote camping widely available throughout Alaska? Sure, but what's notable about the area across the bay are the other options that provide varying degrees of comfort while still giving guests a taste of living in the wild.

At the high end of the spectrum are exclusive getaways like the renowned Kachemak Bay Wilderness Lodge, left, located on its own in a scenic cove. The lodge has a rustic look, but it offers many modern amenities: superb cuisine, a Finnish sauna, a guide service, fresh flowers, fine wines, and other comforts not usually found around the campfire—all for the nonrustic price of more than a thousand dollars a day for two.

It's also a place to begin to get to know Alaska's native art, like the replica totem shown on page 104.

People looking for a compromise between outback camping and the luxurious Kachemak Bay Wilderness Lodge may like places like Peterson Bay Lodge, which costs significantly less than a luxury lodge. The owners of Peterson Bay Lodge divide their time between running the enterprise and tending their oyster farm in the little bay nearby. Many visitors choose to help them haul in and shuck oysters, getting a taste of the homesteading life in the company of a couple who truly live close to the land. Peterson Bay Lodge guests also can partake of subsistence living by hooking a few fish, as can visitors anywhere across Kachemak Bay. Fishing is easily the most popular pastime all across the Kenai Peninsula.

CHAPTER FOUR

Deep into
ALASKA'S INTERIOR

In Alaska's Denali National Park and Preserve, summer sunsets blaze around midnight.

Mount McKinley rises to 20,320 feet, the highest point in North America.

Denali National Park and the Alaskan Interior

M Y COMPANIONS AND I PICKED OUR WAY ALONG THE SPINE OF THE RIDGE, a blade of earth and rock that measured only about six feet across, its sides diving steeply, hundreds of feet to the tundra-covered slopes below. All around us spun the tempestuous summer weather, a polychromatic swirl of gray clouds, silvery curtains of rain, thick shafts of golden light, rainbows, and pools of blue, blue sky. Below us to the north, a brush-lined creek meandered through a green but almost treeless valley. Above us to the south rose the incisor peaks of the robust young Alaska Range. Exhilarated by the flamboyant wildness that enveloped me, I felt I'd never forget my first foray into the backcountry of Denali National Park and Preserve.

And I didn't forget. As I once again headed for Denali in 2005, the wonders of that 1987 trip into the Alaskan interior wafted up from my memory bank. I drove the 237 miles north from Anchorage to the park, remembering the grizzlies, the glaciers, the golden eagles, and that glorious summer afternoon on the ridge.

My visions of Denali's grand wildness temporarily dimmed as I neared the park. In the 18 years since my previous visit, the stretch of the Parks Highway just outside Denali's entrance had sprouted many new hotels, gas stations, fast-food joints, and souvenir shops. True, most of the development adhered to a pseudo-rustic, log-cabin style, but still the strip didn't exactly offer the wilderness experience for which I yearned. I turned into the park, and the crowds didn't diminish. Hundreds of thousands of people enter here every summer. But commercial enterprises did give way to the beautiful new visitor center, the frontcountry campgrounds, and other park facilities—a step in the right direction.

The fastest way to see the wilds would have been to take to the air with one of the "flightseeing" operations based near the park entrance. Due to the expense—$100 to $200 an hour—I passed this time, but in 1987 I had spent a couple of hours in a four-seater, winging over Denali. We had taken off from a gravel landing strip and headed straight for 20,320-foot Mount McKinley, the highest peak in North America. Locals simply refer to it as "the Mountain." On the way we passed over seemingly endless expanses of rolling tundra and boreal forest. Some six million acres, the park is larger than Massachusetts.

Once in the vicinity of Mount McKinley, which remained hidden by clouds, we spiraled up toward its western flank, a gnat approaching an elephant. At about 10,000 feet we emerged from the gray pall and found ourselves face-to-face with the Mountain, its snowy slopes gleaming in the sunlight. Bush planes don't have pressurized cabins, so we couldn't go as high as the summit. We leveled off at 11,000 feet and skirted the massive peak. From its south side, we banked into the maze of ice-shrouded Alaska Range mountains, any one of which might have been called "the Mountain" if it weren't for McKinley's overwhelming presence: 14,573-foot Mount Hunter and 17,400-foot Mount Foraker. Like one of the park's golden eagles, we winged down rugged valleys, gazing at ridges below, lofty summits above, and sheer rock faces beside us, some less than 50 yards away as the pilot steered in for close-ups. As we turned to head home, we flew low over Peters Glacier, staring down into its aqua-tinged crevasses.

Yes, flightseeing offered considerable charms, but my 2005 exploration was to be a more pedestrian affair—literally, not figuratively. I began on the five short trails that wind through the entrance area, which are just about the only established trails in Denali. For the most part these routes pass through the boreal forest or taiga ("land of little sticks" in Russian), the word used for the conifer woods in the cold, harsh belt that circles the globe just south of the treeless Arctic tundra. Many taiga forests consist of scrawny, stunted trees, but there in the Nenana River Valley near the park entrance the spruce grow to substantial sizes, maybe 60 to 80 feet tall and a couple of feet in diameter. Where fires or disease have knocked back the spruce, the early colonizing aspen have moved in, their light green leaves and white bark in bright contrast to the dark, brooding spruce that dominate this system.

My favorite of these five paths was the Mount Healy Overlook Trail, 4.5 miles up and back with a 1,700-foot vertical gain. The trail headed off the main road into a sea of spruce, then entered a large aspen stand. The forest blossomed with bluebells, dogwood, cinquefoil, and prickly rose. I noticed that many of the aspens bore scars where hungry moose had peeled off strips of bark to munch during the winter, when more savory fare is scarce.

Though I was hiking in summer, I knew that moose still might be found along the watercourses. I stayed alert, both because I hoped to see a moose and because I didn't want to blunder into one at close quarters. Cuddly Bullwinkles they are not. Many Alaskans will tell you that they fear moose more than they do bears. Moose are notoriously ornery and, if annoyed, they will try to kick the stuffing out of you. They're fast and they're big— really big. I once stumbled upon a pair of resting bulls, and when they sprang to their hooves, I had to crane my neck to look up at them. I reckon each weighed at least a thousand pounds and stood seven feet at the shoulder, which means the tops of their enormous palmate antlers towered about ten feet off the ground. Needless to say, I backed away quickly and, thankfully, they allowed me to keep my stuffing.

About two-thirds of the way to the Mount Healy overlook, the trail became seriously steep. I found plenty of reasons to take rest stops along the way, such as a foraging marmot and sloping meadows chock-a-block with wildflowers. The trees thinned out, then vanished, due to the park's extreme northern latitude. Timberline lies at about 3,000 feet, compared with a tree line of about 11,000 feet in the Colorado Rockies. By the time I reached the lookout, at 3,425 feet, the vegetation had shrunk to patches of ground-hugging tundra plants interspersed with bare, rocky soil, creating wide-open vistas of the Nenana River Valley and the surrounding mountains.

The views from the Mount Healy overlook are mighty fine, but the eye-popping parts of Denali lie to the west, in the backcountry. The delineation between front- and back-country is artificially sharp because unrestricted public access is limited on the 90-mile main road and, with a few exceptions, only park buses are allowed beyond mile 15. This controls the number of visitors and vehicles, ensures that all the backcountry vehicles are driven by people who understand and respect wildlife, and prevents accidents on the narrow gravel road that twists and tightropes along the edges of precipitous drop-offs.

At six-something one morning, about 20 of us visitors boarded the first park bus of the day. I grabbed a seat on the left side of the bus, having been advised that the lion's share of the sights would be to the south. Unfettered by clouds, the early morning sun shafted through the spruce trees that embraced the road, heralding a blue-sky day. Of course, within a few hours, drizzling rain or even thunderstorms might turn that blue to gray. Our driver, Dick Merrill, gave his introductory spiel. Sounding uncannily like W. C. Fields (though I'm sure Merrill is much nicer to children), he described his rules for wildlife sightings. He would not stop for "dots"—animals so distant that you'd need a telescope to tell a moose from a goose. He would only make "quality" stops, to see notable critters reasonably close to the road. For example, he said, the previous day he'd cut the engine for half an hour to let passengers watch wolves hunt down snowshoe hares. Wolves! For decades I'd futilely scanned North American landscapes in hopes of seeing a wolf. I sat up a little straighter in my seat and made sure my binoculars lay close at hand. (We didn't spot any wolves that day, but I'm delighted to report that a few days later I did see my first wild wolf, a black-coated male that trotted by so close to the bus that I could have dropped my binoculars on him.)

Within minutes we saw a snowshoe hare. I got a good look at those clown-shoe-sized hind feet that allow these hares to scoot across snow without sinking in. They're also known as varying hares because their dark brown summer coats turn white in winter. Soon I saw another snowshoe hare, and another, and another, and at least a dozen more by the time we'd gone five miles. Famous among wildlife biologists for their wildly vacillating populations, the hares clearly were in the midst of one of their upswings, when they may

Climbers head toward the summit of Mount McKinley,

a grueling ascent that hundreds attempt each year.

number more than 2,000 per square mile. During downswings their numbers crash to fewer than 50 in the same area.

Just shy of mile 10 Merrill pulled over, stopped the bus, and directed our attention to the southwest. There it was: the Mountain. At a distance of 70 miles and largely blocked by much closer peaks, it didn't exactly loom, but it still stood out. Strange as it may seem, the odds of getting a clear view of Mount McKinley are probably worse than the odds of seeing the park's second most popular sight, a grizzly, because summer weather tends toward overcast. The sheer mass of McKinley creates its own local weather as well, and often obscures some or all of the peak even when the sun is shining elsewhere in the park.

AT MILE 15 WE CROSSED THE SAVAGE RIVER, THE BOUNDARY THAT PRIVATE VEHICLES generally aren't allowed to pass. The pavement gave way to gravel, symbolic evidence that we were leaving civilization behind. As we proceeded to the Sanctuary and Teklanika Rivers and on to the Igloo and Cathedral Mountains, the road often climbed above timberline, conveniently presenting us with unobstructed views of the wildlife at every turn.

First, we spotted a caribou about 50 yards off the road. It struck me as odd that the beast was lying on the ground with its head buried in a bush, but Merrill said it was probably seeking respite from the flies that sometimes plague these creatures. About a mile later we saw three caribou lounging on a snow bank, which also would provide some relief from bugs as well as from the heat. To a far-north animal like the caribou, 75° F constituted a scorcher. Next came a group of four Dall's sheep, all ewes and lambs. Merrill said that he rarely sees rams during the summer, when the males stay way back in the high country except to migrate with herds from one mountain range to another. Soon we saw another group of ewes and lambs, about a dozen altogether. We stopped to watch these milk-white herbivores graze in the mountain meadows they prefer. It's not that they couldn't find appealing food on the flats, but they generally stay on or near steep slopes, because their primary defense against predators is their climbing prowess. Dall's sheep can run up a mountainside that'd have us humans reaching for ropes and carabiners. Finally, we saw our first grizzlies, a pair of young adults moseying across a tundra-coated hill. Unfortunately, they were about half a mile away, nearly qualifying them as dots in Merrill's eyes, so we only tarried a minute to watch them.

During this wildlife binge—somewhere between the sheep and the grizzlies— a couple of backpackers flagged us down. Their appearance demonstrates how the park's bus system helps, not hinders, their style of independent exploration. Visitors can get on and off the buses at many points along the road. Day hikers and overnight backpackers can use the service, but each step they take off the road is a step into the wilderness. Even people who plan to catch another bus in an hour or two should be well prepared for sun, cold, mosquitoes, storms, bears, and all the other hazards of the Alaskan outdoors.

*This 1905 cabin served as the office of the mining claims recordkeeper in the Kantishna Hills,
at the western end of Denali National Park and Preserve. That year, word of a gold strike
brought thousands of stampeders to these hills, but the rush fizzled almost as quickly
as it started, and by spring of 1906 only about 50 miners remained. The cabin fell into disuse
and eventually was moved to its current site on the grounds of the Kantishna Roadhouse.*

Park tour buses motor over Polychrome Pass along the only road

that penetrates the backcountry of Denali National Park and Preserve.

About 45 miles into the drive we began the long, twisting climb to Polychrome Pass. Though in general I recommend getting a seat with a south-facing window as the bus creeps along the hillside high above the broad valley of the East Fork Toklat River, any passenger who is afraid of heights may want to shift to the other side. We nonphobic passengers, however, crowded to the south-facing windows and relished the views of the braided river, the tundra-greened foothills, and the glacier-streaked peaks of the Alaska Range, not even ten miles away. In the sunlight the many colors of the soil shone brightly, displaying bands of orange, lavender, yellow, white, and black—hence "polychrome."

Merrill had told us not to expect to see Dall's rams in the summer, but just past Polychrome Pass, we got lucky. Not 50 yards from the road we saw four rams resting atop ledges on a cliff overlooking the Toklat River Valley, which they had to cross to reach the Alaska Range. Merrill said they probably were checking out the valley, scanning for wolves and other predators before deciding to brave the flats. These sheep are well-equipped for such scanning; scientists estimate that their vision rivals that of a human looking through eight-power binoculars.

As we sat there admiring the massive, curved horns of the three older rams, a large but sleek bird skimmed into view above the sheep. I raised my binoculars and discerned that it was some kind of raptor, perhaps a falcon. I followed it, noting the largely white body streaked with black, the long tail, and the heavy, muscular build. Could it be? I asked Merrill if I could be looking at a gyrfalcon. Yes, indeed, he said; a pair of gyrfalcons was nesting in the area. I'm not a fanatic birder, but this sighting excited me. I'd never seen a gyrfalcon before; they're uncommon in Alaska and rare in the lower 48. The largest of all falcons, they're known as the king's bird because, in medieval times, they were so prized by falconers that only kings and princes could legally own them. Falconers today still covet them, and sometimes unscrupulous practitioners pay tens of thousands of dollars for gyrfalcons poached from the wild.

As we continued west, we relished more views of the grand landscape and a diverse array of wildlife. At mile 66, where a new visitor center is projected to open in 2007, the view included a clear look at the Mountain, a mere 33 miles distant. But the closest view possible from a place you can reach in a bus came near the end of the road, when Merrill turned off at mile 85 and took us into the Wonder Lake Campground. At the far point of this 28-tent-site spread, Mount McKinley loomed from a mere 27 miles away.

And "loomed" is truly the word. By the time we had parked at Wonder Lake, some clouds had moved in and momentarily obscured the upper portion of the Mountain. I stared hard, waiting for the clouds to part so I could see the summit. The view finally did clear, and I discovered that my upturned gaze was not nearly upturned enough. The line of sight I'd chosen hit the Mountain in its midsection; I had to tilt my head back several more notches before I was looking at the summit. My brain said something like, "Holy cow! What the heck is that mountaintop doing way up there in the sky?"

A naturalist later told me that visitors commonly focus way too low as they search for openings in the clouds to see the summit. That's partly because the Mountain is 20,320 feet high, but it's mainly because it towers some 18,000 feet higher than the lowlands at its base. For comparison's sake, Mount Everest lifts 12,000 feet above its surroundings. Mount McKinley is thought to be one of the world's highest vertical rises, the highest being Nanga Parbat, in India.

As its misty veil slipped away and the full mountain revealed itself, I sat down on a rock and simply gaped. I overheard a woman who was equally transfixed tell her companion, "I just can't stop looking at it." Exactly.

EVENTUALLY I DID HAVE TO CATCH THE BUS FOR THE FINAL FIVE MILES TO MY DESTINATION near the end of the 90-mile road. I was heading for Camp Denali, a venerable place that has been around since 1952, and the place from which I'd ventured forth on the 1987 hike that had taken me to that glorious ridge I mentioned at the start of this chapter. It may seem odd to find a lodge in the middle of the Denali wilderness, but it and two others were grand-fathered into the park when Denali's area was tripled in 1980. The lodges operate under strict rules to minimize their presence and impact. Besides, the folks at Camp Denali are conservation-minded stewards who focus on teaching their guests about the natural won-ders of the park. The camp employs several naturalists who lead outings and, along with occasional guest speakers, give slide shows and lectures about the ecology of forest fires, bears, wildflowers, and other appropriate topics.

Warming yourself by the woodstove in one of the camp's 17 cozy hillside cabins can lull you into thinking you're in some nice, safe, civilized area. But you're not, and it's important to remember that. Case in point: At about five o'clock one morning I headed out on a trail that led to nearby Moose Creek. Not 200 yards down the path I noticed fresh grizzly tracks in the mud—a sow and a cub, judging by the size and stride length. And they were going my way. Knowing that I wouldn't want to come between a protective grizzly mom and her cub unless I was in an armored humvee, I slowed down and started making some noise to alert the bears to my presence. Grizzlies don't like surprises. Another couple of hundred yards down the trail I came to a still-steaming pile of bear scat, which told me I likely was right on the heels of the bears. I promptly did an about-face and marched back to the lodge. Perhaps I'd see the beaver pond on Moose Creek tomorrow.

During my 1987 stay at Camp Denali, back when I didn't know much about the ways of the wild, I found out what can happen when you don't give nature the respect it's due. Camp Denali had (and still has) the unique grandfathered right to keep several canoes just off the road at the north end of Wonder Lake, three miles from the camp-ground, which occupies the lake's south end. Around noon one day I'd gone to the wilderness lake, totally undeveloped except for the campground, to go canoeing by myself without a life vest—a boneheaded beginning to a boneheaded venture. I started paddling south, and within half an hour I'd managed to get a couple of miles down the lake, blithely imbibing the solitude and stark beauty of the landscape.

Many backpackers find their own routes across the tundra of Denali National Park.
Only a handful of trails exist in this vast park, so venturing into the backcountry requires
the ability to navigate in a vast and trackless wilderness.
But those who go off the beaten path enjoy spectacular scenery and solitude.

As often happens in the afternoon—not that I had a clue before it happened—a storm began brewing and the wind began blowing, so I turned around to head home. I thought that, paddling a canoe by myself, I had to take a few strokes on one side, and then a few on the other, or else I would go in a circle. Well, I paddled several times on the right side, which naturally turned the bow slightly to the left, then I prepared to paddle on the left side to straighten out the canoe. But before I could shift, the head wind whipped my canoe around 180 degrees, pointing me due south.

Weird, I thought. But I didn't yet grasp why experienced canoeists worry about the wind. So I turned the canoe around and starting heading north again. Again I paddled several times on the right side, and then began my shift to the left—only this time I moved very quickly, to .... Too late. The wind spun me around again. Hmmm. Maybe if I shifted very, *very* quickly .... Nope. Maybe if I started paddling on the left side instead? I tried it.... Nope. Maybe if I said enough very, very bad words. Nope.

At this point it occurred to me that being stuck alone without a life vest in the middle of a remote lake in a storm surrounded by hypothermia-inducing water was not a good thing. In 1987 I wasn't aware of the campground, so it didn't occur to me to go south with the wind to find help. I contemplated paddling to the shore, ditching the canoe, and bushwhacking through the swampy, mosquito- and grizzly-infested brush. But, assuming I made it to the road, I'd then have to hoof it five miles, plead for help, and go back and somehow retrieve the canoe. Forget that. There had to be a way.

There was, but it wasn't pretty. By trial and error I discovered that if I paddled just twice on one side, and then frantically switched to the other side and paddled just twice there, and then frantically switched back to the first side and paddled just twice there, and then .... You get the idea. That way I usually could keep the canoe straight into the wind, so it wouldn't catch the side of the canoe and push me around.

Usually. But every few minutes the wind would shift direction a little and hit the canoe at a bit of an angle, spinning me once again. To make matters worse, the wind picked up, and once I got turned to the south, it was extremely difficult to paddle hard enough to rotate the canoe back to the north. By the time I'd done this for about the tenth time, my arms had begun to quiver with fatigue, and I hadn't even gone half a mile. Increasingly desperate, I finally hit on a technique that saved my bacon. When a gust spun me, I no longer fought the spin. I'd paddle on the side that would speed up the spin, so the momentum took me full circle and left me pointing north again. Using my crazed methods, I got back to the road in a mere two hours, utterly exhausted and so sore that I hardly could raise my hands to swat mosquitoes as I trudged back to the camp.

I'M GLAD I SURVIVED, THOUGH, BECAUSE OTHERWISE I WOULDN'T HAVE BEEN at Camp Denali in 2005 to go on an all-day cross-country hike with one of the camp naturalists and about ten other guests. After driving back about 20 miles along the park road, we parked and then headed up the slope to the north. We began at 3,400 feet, already above tree line. I felt the spongy, hummocky ground beneath my boots and I knew we were walking on moist tundra, which stays wet because water pools on the permafrost lying a foot or two below the surface. Ankle- and kneehigh blueberries, horsetails, lichens, crowberries, and grasses thrived here. As we ascended, the moist tundra graded into dry tundra, where the vegetation is shorter and less hummocky, making for much easier walking. Many of the hillsides rioted with wildflowers, including pink moss campion, paintbrush, Arctic bell heather, wild geraniums, tiny orchids, purple mountain saxifrage, and blue forget-me-not, Alaska's state flower. In some places, huge chunks of sod had been peeled off by grizzlies digging for Eskimo potatoes, a lovely spring wildflower with edible tubers that people can roast and eat as well.

From a knoll we looked down several hundred yards to a hundred-foot-high rock outcropping on which a pair of golden eagles had built their nest. From our vantage point, we could see one of the fluffy eaglets flapping its little wings, preparing for the day when it would swoop down on Arctic ground squirrels. Presently one of the adults flew in with some kind of dead critter, which it tore into pieces and fed to the voracious youngsters.

We climbed on to a small tundra meadow atop a ridge at about 4,400 feet, where we stopped for lunch. Right below us lay a boulder field that housed a marmot colony. The sun had come out, and through my binoculars I watched a plump male marmot stretch out on a rock, luxuriating in the warmth. An eagle flapped overhead, trying to escape a long-tailed jaeger that was pestering it.

After lunch we lingered, drinking in the immense vistas and scanning the hills and valleys for wildlife. Suddenly, one of the guests let out a yelp and pointed down the north side of the ridge. About 300 yards away, a blonde grizzly had come out from behind some bushes and was feeding on the tundra vegetation. As we watched, another grizzly appeared, then another, and finally one more. The blonde was the mom and the three smaller— but nearly grown-up—bears were her triplet cubs. Probably two-and-a-half years old, our guide figured. It wouldn't be too many months before mom would send them off to fend for themselves and, if all went well, she'd have more cubs.

We spent about half an hour watching the bears rummage around before we packed up and started back to the bus. To descend from the ridge, we headed west along its spine, which grew increasingly narrow until we found ourselves picking our way along a blade of earth and rock measuring only about six feet across.

Suddenly I realized that this was the very ridge on which I'd walked 18 years earlier. Stunned by this realization, memories flooding my reeling mind, I stopped and looked around. I could see it now: the dimly familiar view of the river valley, the hills verging on mountains to the east, the Alaska Range to the south. So much the same, yet so much different—the weather, the grizzlies, the eagles. Denali seemed timeless, and yet at the same time ever changing. Maybe I'd comprehend that apparent contradiction if I visited the park a few more times.

Sounds good to me. I wonder if I could find my way back to that ridge in 2023? ■

Granted a clear view of Mount McKinley and the Alaska Range—
a view obscured more often than not by clouds—a canoeist paddles
on Wonder Lake, about 30 miles north of the Mountain.
The four-mile-long lake lies at the western end of Denali National Park.

Reflected in the quiet waters of Wonder Lake, the icebound peaks of

the Alaska Range rise above lowlands in Denali National Park.

Putting nature's pieces together

Denali National Park is one of those expanses

of Alaskan wilderness that has it all:

wildlife galore, dazzling vistas, forest and tundra,

enormous glaciers, and hefty mountains,

topped off by the continent's highest peak.

But Denali also reveals the workings of the wild,

the processes and relationships that keep nature running.

No one knows exactly how all the pieces of the wilderness fit together, but when you travel through Denali, you feel that it all makes sense.

The beauty and harmony of the place suggest the presence of a scrupulous system in which the birds and the rivers and the bugs mesh and form a community greater than the sum of its parts.

Take fireweed, the wildflower shown on page 130. It isn't just another pretty face, though its red-pink-purple blossoms certainly beautify the landscape during the summer. Fireweed is an important pioneer species that moves into disturbed areas following catastrophic events such as forest fires—hence the plant's name. The rapid appearance of fireweed prevents erosion while creating a sunny, open area that diversifies the habitat of the landscape.

The tundra found throughout most of Denali, opposite, demonstrates the tight relationship of the park's plants and its climate. Ground-hugging berry species, upper right, three-inch-tall willows, and stunted sedges all are adapted to survive interior Alaska's rough winters. Plants foolhardy enough to grow above Denali's surprisingly thin snowpack get flayed by Arctic winds.

Denali's fauna further demonstrate the subtle order characterizing this wilderness. Consider the division of labor. Red foxes, below right, prey on the little things, such as Arctic ground squirrels, hares, mice, and even insects. At the other end of the continuum, grizzly bears, preceding page, are the top predators and seek big targets, such as moose and caribou.

There is some overlap, however. Grizzlies crave Arctic ground squirrels, for example, and will devote hours to excavating their burrows. And sometimes the threads of the tapestry become densely interwoven, as when a ground squirrel gets much-needed salts by gnawing on the antlers of a caribou that was killed by a grizzly.

Nature that
GOES ON FOREVER

Mount Logan, Canada's tallest peak at 19,524 feet, juts out of an icefield in Kluane National Park.

Gray wolves prowl the wilderness of Kluane National Park and Reserve and Tatshenshini-Alsek Provincial Park.

Kluane National Park and Tatshenshini-Alsek Provincial Park

A RE YOU FEELING THE URGE TO GET AS FAR AS POSSIBLE FROM BURGER KINGS and traffic jams, cell phones and TVs? I know just the place. It's the planet's largest international protected area. Some 24 million acres in size—that's bigger than Indiana—this remote natural haven, included on UNESCO's World Heritage List, sprawls across the intersection of the Yukon, British Columbia, and Alaska and includes Kluane National Park and Reserve and Tatshenshini-Alsek Provincial Park in Canada, plus Glacier Bay and Wrangell–St. Elias National Parks and Preserves in Alaska.

I began a recent visit to the Canadian portion of this wilderness by driving west on the Alaska Highway into Haines Junction, deep in the southwest corner of the Yukon. In this small town the highway makes a 90-degree turn and heads northwest. When I looked at a topographical map, I immediately understood why: Southwest of Haines Junction there rises a vast expanse of mountains and icefields that scared the road into changing course. The portion of that intimidating expanse closest to Haines Junction lies within Kluane National Park.

In fact, jagged mountains and icefields constitute about 80 percent of Kluane. Like volcanoes stabbing from the ocean, skyscraping peaks tower above the sea of ice, topped by 19,524-foot Mount Logan, Canada's loftiest summit and the second-highest point of land in North America. Kluane's Ice Age backcountry is generally left to mountaineers, though visitors who don't know a crampon from a piton can tour this harsh land in a small plane or even stay overnight by traveling with an outfit that maintains a camp on the ice.

Like 99-plus percent of the people who come to Kluane, I did not venture into the icefields or stand triumphantly atop Mount Logan. I was content to poke around in the million acres of frontcountry along the park's eastern boundary. But don't let the word "front-country" fool you; this is no city park. It is a nearly untouched land of forested valleys, swift rivers, and rugged mountains, though the latter peak out at about 7,000 feet instead of 19,524.

I decided to sample the dozen or so trails that slip into the frontcountry from its eastern perimeter. I started with the Rock Glacier Trail because I wanted to find out what the heck a rock glacier is. A 30-minute amble through marsh and forest put me on a hillside where I got my answer. The trail ended amid a jumble of gray, tan, and red rocks—the snout of a rock glacier. Interpretive signs explained that this uncommon landform began with 8,000 years of freezing and thawing, which shattered the bedrock of the steep peaks into fragments. Lubricated by meltwater and riding a core of glacial ice, this growing mass of rock slowly flowed down the mountain. What else could one call it but a rock glacier?

Another day I explored a more traditional slice of Kluane by tramping up and back on the six-mile, round-trip King's Throne Trail. It started out on the Cottonwood Trail at comely Kathleen Lake, winding through a forest of white spruce, balsam poplar, and aspen, sprinkled with wildflowers. I also noted the abundance of soapberry bushes. When the berries are ripe, both grizzly and black bears descend on this place; an adult bear can pack away 200,000 soapberries in a day. As I passed the berry patches I spotted several trees with claw marks and hairs left behind by bears that had scratched their backs on the bark.

After a mile or so I split off onto the King's Throne Trail proper. Don't miss the turn unless you're carrying gear and supplies for a week; the Cottonwood Trail continues as a 50-mile loop. I headed up the moderate grade through the forest for about a mile, then emerged from the trees into the big-sky country of the alpine tundra. From there the path tilted upward in a series of quadriceps-burning switchbacks, but the higher I climbed, the better the views, so I reckon the 1,600-foot vertical gain was worth the effort.

The longest hike I took, Slims East, is classified in the Kluane literature as a route, not a trail: a cross-country trek without any established path. I went with a park natural-ist and four other visitors. I figured they'd be good company, and I wanted to benefit from the wealth of information that naturalists provide. Going with a group answered my safety concerns, too. Slims East is known as prime grizzly territory, and as our naturalist told us, he'd never heard of a grizzly attacking a group of four or more. Good thing, as it turned out.

We headed out along the east bank of the Slims River, traipsing through conifer forests, reedy wetlands, and willow thickets along the river. At times we had to ease across fast-moving creeks whose icy water soaked us up to our shins. Thank goodness it was a sunny day. After several hours we paused at a gravel bar for lunch, then headed back.

The bear got remarkably close before we saw it, considering that it was an adult male grizzly that stood about seven feet tall and probably weighed 500 pounds. As we were passing through a sparse patch of forest near the river, one of the other visitors emitted a strange little sound and pointed vigorously. We followed the line of sight indicated by his jabbing finger and saw the bear in the trees about one hundred feet away, moving sideways to us. Sideways wasn't as good as away, but it was much better than toward.

Following standard bear-repelling procedure, which the naturalist had discussed, we clustered together and spoke loudly to the bear, clearly identifying ourselves as humans—it wouldn't do to have the bear mistake us for porterhouse steaks or such. We also waved our arms and raised our day packs or coats above our heads in an attempt to look big. The naturalist and I were packing heat—bear spray, sort of like mace on steroids—so we unholstered our spray cans and pulled out the safety pins, just in case.

The grizzly didn't come closer, but it didn't go farther, either. It continued circling us, occasionally standing on its hind feet and sniffing the air. The naturalist told us, in a reasonably calm voice, that when the bear reared up like that it was checking us out with its eyes and nose, trying to decide just what to do about us. We kept waving and talking and bulking up. Then the grizzly suddenly dropped to all fours, and in seconds it was gone.

Had it picked up an offensive odor from us? Had one of us said something particularly scary? Or did it finally realize that we were a group of more than four and therefore off-limits? Our naturalist just shrugged. We'd never know why the bear left so abruptly, he said, but we knew we were glad it had. Of course, once those forbidding teeth and claws were out of sight, we talked about how great it had been to have such a close look at a grizzly. I sure was glad I'd gone out with a group.

A naturalist who lived in a remote area not far from Kluane told me about an incident that demonstrated the degree of forbearance that grizzlies can display. The deck of her house hung over a small gravel beach. Occasionally grizzlies passed along this stretch of beach, sending her golden retriever into paroxysms of barking from the safety of the deck. However, one time during a bear alert the dog rushed off to confront the interloper. It turned out to be two interlopers—a sow and her cub, a potentially lethal combination. Standing on the deck, the naturalist screamed at her dog to return to the house, but the retriever wasn't about to pass up on the barking opportunity of a lifetime, so it stood about ten yards from the bears and let fly. The sow tolerated this for a little while, but inevitably her protective instincts kicked in and, with fearsome speed, she closed on the dog and pinned it to the ground beneath a giant front paw. The frantic naturalist saw the grizzly clamp it jaws on the head of the trapped dog and knew her beloved pet would soon be barking at angels.

But the mama bear didn't bite down. She held the dog's head in her mouth for a few seconds, as if teaching this rude animal a lesson, and then released it, unharmed. She and her cub then departed while the dazed retriever wobbled to its feet and stared after them. Now, golden retrievers typically don't learn lessons quickly, and this one was no exception. After its head cleared—as much as it ever would—the dog resumed barking and ran after the bears, which had disappeared into the forest. The dog disappeared after them, and the naturalist felt sure the grizzly wouldn't give the dog a second chance. But apparently the bear did, because after a few minutes the retriever returned, trotting in that upright way that radiates canine pride. The dog was claiming victory, telling the world that it had run off those pesky bears. The relieved naturalist welcomed her dog back into the house and looked it over for wounds, but found nothing. The bear encounter had produced one dreadful result, however: The dog's head was drenched in bear saliva, which is on the universe's top-ten list of rank-smelling substances.

Even though Kluane Lake lies along the highway,

few visitors get there in winter to see it partly iced over.

If hiking in the Kluane frontcountry whets your appetite for even more wildness, there is one way to travel at ground level through the heart of the 24-million-acre sanctuary of which Kluane is a part. You need only drive 52 miles south on the highway from Haines Junction, take a god-awful dirt access road a few miles to its end in the ghost town of Dalton Post, board a raft, and head down the Tatshenshini River. The Tat winds through Tatshenshini-Alsek Provincial Park and joins the Alsek River just shy of the American border. The combined river flows across the international boundary into Glacier Bay National Park and drops rafters at Dry Bay, on the Pacific Coast, where people can catch a plane back to civilization. This is the only river route that cuts through the lofty Coast Mountains. Many river rats call this one of the world's ten best wilderness raft trips.

A few years ago I floated down the Tat-Alsek with four others who had been hired to survey the area to help determine the quality of its bear habitat: two wildlife researchers, Anne Weerstra and Richard Roth; an aquatic ecologist, Darwin Monita; and our boatman, Craig Corona. On a slightly overcast July morning, Corona rowed our heavily laden raft out into the gray-green glacier-fed river until the current seized us and hauled us downstream. Within one minute we left all traces of development behind; we wouldn't see signs of civilization again until we reached Dry Bay, ten days later.

We swooshed past banks bristling with willows, balsam poplar, and the dominant spruce. A number of stumps bore the marks of beaver teeth, but we saw none of those industrious rodents nor any other mammals that day, though we probably would have if the vegetation hadn't been so thick it would hide a herd of elephants. Birds we saw: kingfishers, far-ranging Arctic terns (they winter in the Southern Hemisphere), merganser mothers trailing fuzzy little ducklings, a colony of cliff swallows, and bald eagles. Lots and lots of bald eagles; they were as abundant as crows in a corn field.

Later that day the Tat squeezed through a long canyon, giving us a Class 3 whitewater ride. Loosely translated, Class 3 means rapids that elevate your pulse and put a grin on your face but don't present serious danger as long as your skipper knows what he's doing. And Corona definitely knew what he was doing. That was the last significant whitewater we encountered. The rest of the way, the Tat-Alsek is a broad, reasonably smooth river.

On day three the team started its bear research in earnest. They would note any bear sightings and signs of bear activity—such as the tracks we spotted on nearly every sandbar and mud bank we stopped at—but their main work was systematically surveying vegetation at designated spots to determine how well the flora would support grizzly and black bears. So early that morning Weerstra, Roth, and I trooped up to the top of a riverside bluff and navigated our way to the first spot on the map. The two researchers marked off an area of about 12 by 12 yards—three-hundredths of an acre—and began sifting through the dense vegetation, identifying plant species and estimating the abundance of each.

They finished in half an hour, so we set off for the next site, about 250 yards away. As we waded through the forest understory we began yelling, just as we'd done on our way

This barren-ground caribou has just started to grow its antlers, which eventually
will develop into a magnificent rack. Unlike any others in the deer family,
both males and females of this species sport antlers. Every year tens of thousands
of barren-ground caribou migrate through Canada's Yukon.

The bald eagle may be the national bird of the United States, but these glorious birds

also frequent Canada's Kluane National and Tatshenshini-Alsek Provincial Parks.

You can bet that somewhere not far away a big, strong, fiercely protective

cow moose is keeping a watchful eye over these two calves.

A few hikers get to see the Alsek Glacier from the land. It is more often viewed from the water, where its seven-mile-long face, together with the neighboring Grand Plateau Glacier, looms along the edge of the Alsek River, greeting rafters as they near the end of their 140-mile run down the Tatshenshini-Alsek.

up to the top of the bluff, just as we did whenever we went anywhere farther than from the campfire to our tents. We wanted to let any bears in the vicinity know that we were coming. The three of us were adequate shouters, but we missed Monita, who had perfected a resonant *DAAAYYYYY-OOOOOO* that sounded just like the opening to the famous "Banana Boat Song." When I asked him why, Monita said, "Bears really dislike Harry Belafonte."

Yes, we were scrupulous about yelling—while on the move. But while we were at the plots, we stopped shouting and focused on the work, the unconscious assumption being that only when *we* were traveling was there the possibility of encountering a bear. Bad assumption. As Weerstra and Roth were wrapping up the third plot and I was sitting against a tree taking notes, Weerstra suddenly blurted "Omigod!" and scrambled backward a few steps to where I was sitting. A scant 15 feet from us stood a black bear that had blundered into our plot, almost colliding with Weerstra. It looked as startled as we did.

Weerstra stared at the bear, Roth looked over to see what was happening, and I fumbled at my holstered bear spray for a few moments before I finally got it out and yanked the safety pin. I guess I should have spent more time practicing my quick draw before this point. For about the count of five, it was a standoff. Then the bear turned tail and bounded off through the undergrowth in an unnerving display of speed and agility. In a few seconds, it was gone. From that point on, Weerstra and Roth conducted the loudest vegetation surveys on record.

The designated spots for laying out the veg plots had been chosen to produce a scientific sampling, not for their accessibility, and that made for some tough hiking, as we discovered the following day. The morning dawned cold and clear except for the mantle of fog draped over the mountaintops. We rafted a few miles to the mouth of a creek, where we pulled out and headed up a steep slope toward the next site. Anticipating some fairly hard bushwhacking, we reckoned it would take us about an hour to cover the mile and a half to the spot. An hour later we'd gone maybe 400 yards.

Not only was the vegetation a tightly woven tangle, but it was strengthened by a sturdy framework of shrubby alder, the way concrete is reinforced by metal rods. Plowing through this green wall was like doing a third-and-one fullback plunge into the defensive line of the Green Bay Packers, over and over and over. We had to slither through holes, clamber over the top, and keep those legs driving as we bulled forward. And it seemed as if everything growing amid the alder slashed and stung. "It's like they put all the worst plants in the world on this hill," said Roth as we cursed the prickly rose, red raspberry, devil's club, and stinging nettles. We dubbed those four menaces plus alder the "Big Five": the components, along with steep slopes and mosquitoes, of a trophy-level hike.

After another hour and another 400 yards, we collapsed in a little meadow atop a knob, panting and dripping sweat. Not even halfway. We stared across a Big Five–infested ravine and up the far slope to our goal. No way. Weerstra and Roth surveyed a plot next to the meadow and used a spotting scope to make a cursory study of the vegetation at the designated site. We were not the first visitors, nor would we be the last, to have our plans foiled by the raw nature of the Tat-Alsek.

For several more days we plotted our way down the Tat, watching for mountain goats, listening to Corona recite Coyote folktales by the campfire, and bumping into bears. (Oh, yeah, we did indeed have other close encounters of the furred kind, including a run-in with a sow and two cubs that had the mom huffing at us—a sign of serious agitation that sent us packing.) About 90 miles down the Tat, we came to the confluence with the Alsek River, about 10 miles from the U.S. border. More than a mile wide in places, the path of the combined river led west, a sprawl of braided channels and gravel bars. Thousands and thousands of feet above the river spread the broad shoulders of the St. Elias Mountains, dozens of glaciers spilling down their flanks.

WE CAMPED ONE NIGHT ON A LITTLE ISLAND IN THE MIDDLE OF THE CONFLUENCE, our tents set amid lush meadows of larkspur, kneeling angelica, and radiantly fuchsia fireweed that grew taller than our heads. Close by we saw the fresh tracks of a grizzly sow and her cubs. Bald eagles and Arctic terns winged overhead. Voles and mice hustled through the underbrush. And everywhere, enveloping us and everything else in the valley, there sounded the music of the rivers as they strummed the earth, their waters forever cycling, at once rushing away from this spot and rushing back to it.

The team's survey was over, and we hightailed it downriver to Dry Bay. But during this final couple of days we still feasted on the grand landscape, particularly the river's-edge glaciers—appropriate, as we had entered Glacier Bay National Park as soon as we crossed the border. About 15 miles into the park we floated past miles of Novatak Glacier. Chunks of the glacier that had broken off accompanied us down the river—icebergs of varying sizes and shades of blue bobbing along next to us in the current. Decidedly surreal. However, Corona kept us at least 50 feet from any bergs whose visible portion was bigger than, say, a Ford Explorer, in case they flipped over. It wouldn't do to have that famously larger below-the-tip-of-the-iceberg portion rise up under the raft. That water looked cold.

Like running with the bulls at Pamplona, we ran with the bergs, traveling among them for about ten miles until the river suddenly ballooned into the several square miles of Alsek Lake, an extremely wide spot in the river that lay beneath the icy, seven-mile-wide face of the Alsek and Grand Plateau Glaciers. Taking turns, we rowed through the almost still water, watching pieces of ice, some the size of houses, break off the glaciers and splash into the lake. The crack of the splitting ice reverberated across the water like a cannon shot.

The river narrowed, and the current picked up and swept us back to civilization in a few hours. Nothing but a few small fish processing plants, some scattered cabins, and the gravel landing strip where our plane awaited, but it seemed like Manhattan after ten days in the wilderness. I found myself wishing that rafts could travel upriver. The researchers had concluded that the Tat-Alsek harbored plenty of outstanding bear habitat. I'd concluded that it harbored plenty of outstanding country for human visitors, too. ∎

*In autumn, fireweed blazes with colors that justify its name, though it actually
was so named because it quickly colonizes land after a fire burns off the previous vegetation.
Known better for its fuchsia summer blooms than its bright orange autumn foliage,
fireweed grows throughout most of western Canada.*

Even in the far northern reaches of Canada, it gets warm enough

during the summer to melt the snow and ice.

Getting there

The hoary cliché "Getting there is half the fun" rings true

for travel in Kluane National Park and Tatshenshini-Alsek

Provincial Park. It's not like laboring to get somewhere

by slogging through traffic on a city street

or wedging into a packed commercial airliner.

In the backcountry of the Far North, the adventure begins

as soon as you take your first step.

When you fly from Houston to Pittsburgh, you read a book, do some work, or hope there's a decent in-flight movie. But when you get into a helicopter to fly to a viewpoint above the Kaskawulch Glacier in Kluane National Park, right, it is guaranteed that you will not pull out your laptop to go over the latest sales figures. If you depart from Haines Junction, the flight out to the glacier will take you over the park's heavily forested lowlands, the 5,000-foot peaks of the frontcountry range, the broad river valleys of the upper Alsek system, and the aqua fissures of the glacier itself.

Often getting there is even more than half the fun—more like 99 percent—because the journey is the point of it all. People who hike the Cottonwood Trail, for instance, had better pay attention and enjoy the sights along the way instead of waiting to find something at the end, because this 50-mile trail is a loop. Similarly, to climb the ice around the Lowell Glacier, page 156, is to relish the challenge of ascending an ice pinnacle, not to perch or picnic atop it.

The raft trip down the Tatshenshini and Alsek Rivers, right, and through Tatshenshini-Alsek Provincial Park is absolutely, 100 percent about the journey. The end of the line is nothing more than a remote airstrip from which to fly home.

But during the 140 miles it takes to get there, the river passes through sublime wilderness, part of the largest international protected area on the planet. Rafters float past red-purple fields of head-high fireweed, sandbars pocked by grizzly tracks, massive glaciers calving icebergs into the river, bald eagles feasting on salmon, and peaks whose summits disappear into the clouds. You'll want to bring binoculars, but leave the latest Grisham novel back home.

CHAPTER SIX

Highway to the
FAR NORTH AND FARTHER

Two highways traverse the Arctic Circle: Alaska's Dalton Highway, above, and Canada's Dempster Highway.

When the Arctic ice melts, polar bears come ashore in the far northern reaches of Alaska and Canada.

HIGHWAY TO THE FAR NORTH AND FARTHER

The Dempster Highway

NOTHING ELSE WAS ON MY SCHEDULE THAT DAY, SO I FIGURED I MIGHT AS WELL drive to the Arctic. Okay, I wasn't quite that spontaneous, but I could have been. Sitting in that gas station in the Yukon, all I had to do was exit the station, turn left, and head north. Surprisingly simple, given that in most people's minds, traveling to the Arctic involves icebreakers and dog sleds.

Only two roads in North America cross the Arctic Circle. One is the Dalton Highway in Alaska, which connects the oil fields of Prudhoe Bay to the state's main road system. The other is the road I was about to explore: the Dempster Highway. This 456-mile byway branches north off the Klondike Highway about 25 miles east of Dawson, in the west-central part of the Yukon. It passes over the Arctic Circle after 252 miles, continues northeast, then crosses into the northwest corner of the Northwest Territories, slides up the east side of the Mackenzie River delta, and ends in the little town of Inuvik, about 50 miles short of the Arctic Ocean.

Turning left onto the Dempster and heading north may be simple, but simple isn't necessarily the same as easy. Motorists shouldn't take the Dempster lightly. Other than the first five and last six miles, the road is gravel. It has ruts and bumps and potholes. It gets slick when it's too wet and, oddly, when it's too dry— the dust gets so thick that it's almost like driving on snow. I drove the Dempster in a rented Toyota Corolla, but I definitely had to take it easy. I would have preferred a four-wheel drive, high-clearance vehicle.

Highway though it is, the Dempster runs through a remote and wild stretch of North America. In 456 miles you'll encounter no more than three tiny settlements, only two of which offer gas, food, and basic car repair. Such remoteness magnifies mishaps; an incident that would be a minor annoyance at home, such as a flat tire, becomes a major headache if you're not prepared. If you get stranded during the cold months—and that's most of them—you're talking about a life-threatening situation. But you'll escape with your life during the summer when it's 50° or 60° F and another vehicle is likely to come along in half an hour or so. Still, I'd recommend carrying an extra spare tire, ample food and water, warm clothing (you could hit snow in the passes), basic tools, and a jerry can of gas. Of course, this is one of those do-as-I-say-not-as-I-do situations. I brought the food, the water, and the warm clothing, but I didn't bring any of the other things. Hey, what can I say? For some reason the airline balked when I wanted to bring a spare, a screwdriver set, and a ten-gallon can of gas onto the plane as carry-on luggage.

I FILLED UP MY GAS TANK IN DEMPSTER CORNER—THE INFORMAL NAME GIVEN to the service station/garage/motel/restaurant cluster at the junction of the Klondike and the Dempster Highways. Then I took a deep breath, made that decisive left turn, and started driving toward the Arctic.

For the first 40 miles or so the road snaked through the spruce and poplar of the boreal forest, but then it started climbing and the woods began thinning. After a few miles the highway elevated to about 4,000 feet above sea level, and the trees vanished. I had entered the tundra world, where the icy hand of winter grips the landscape so long and so hard that very little grows any higher than your knees. Except for a few places in which the highway descended into forested, low-elevation river valleys, I'd be in the wide-open tundra the rest of the way.

Another geographical fact reinforced the sense that around mile 40 I'd passed into the Arctic region. The Continental Divide runs through this area. Water on the south side flows into the Yukon River system and ends up in the Pacific Ocean, whereas water on the north side flows into the Mackenzie River system and ends up in the Arctic Ocean.

At this point the Dempster enters Tombstone Territorial Park, a prime cut of the Ogilvie Mountains through which the road passes for some 40 miles. Most dramatic are the craggy black peaks and ridges whose lower slopes are painted tundra green. At mile 46 I stopped at an overlook to admire this landscape, including needle-nosed Tombstone Mountain, the highest peak along the highway, 7,195 feet tall.

While scanning with my binoculars, I spotted a group of bright, white animals lounging in a high mountain meadow: Dall's sheep, close kin to the bighorn sheep of the lower 48. These ewes and lambs were stationary, engaged in the vital but dull act of chewing their cuds, but when they're on the move, Dall's sheep use their hooves to ascend nearly vertical rocky slopes, slopes that would scare off most humans despite our flexible fingers and opposable thumbs. I've seen young lambs hone their climbing skills by clambering atop their moms, creating an oh-how-cute image, though probably bruising their moms in the process.

Five miles farther along I pulled over at the summit of 4,265-foot North Fork Pass, the literal high point of the highway. I hiked up an adjacent knoll to have a closer look at this southern enclave of high Arctic tundra. Nothing knee-high here; these plants were all ankle-biters, the kind of ground-hugging vegetation one usually finds a couple of hundred miles farther north. It grows here partly due to the elevation and partly because the shape of the land funnels frigid Arctic air right through. Just inches below the surface lies permafrost, which forces plants to make do with shallow roots. But they manage. I knelt down to examine the lowbush cranberry, Labrador tea, bearberry, and other bonsai-size shrubs. Moss campion, sweet coltsfoot, and other low-lying wildflowers added brilliant colors to the green carpet.

AFTER DESCENDING FROM NORTH FORK PASS, THE ROAD MORE OR LESS LEVELED out at about mile 55 and the landscape smoothed from jagged peaks to the rolling hills of the Blackstone Uplands. Lush in a stark, far-north sort of way, the Blackstone Uplands surround the Dempster for about 30 miles. I slowed to maybe 20 miles per hour—not because the road was particularly bad but because these uplands teem with wildlife. Instead of paying attention to my driving, I was eyeing the tundra for critters. (If anyone mentions this to my daughter, who just got her driver's license and has endured many righteous lectures on cautious driving from me, I'll deny everything.)

Within a few minutes I spied a pair of trumpeter swans. I stopped to watch these huge white birds glide around a shallow pond, occasionally stretching their slender necks to nibble some aquatic vegetation or perhaps a tasty insect. One of the swans also spent some time preening. In adapting the word "preen" into our everyday vocabulary, it has come to describe someone vain and self-satisfied who is fussing over his appearance, but this metaphorical usage impugns the character of swans and other avian preeners. For them, preening is a matter of survival, not vanity. The swan I saw was preening by smearing oil from a gland near its rump onto its bill, then rubbing the oil into its feathers. The oil protects its feathers and provides insulation against the cold, and some scientists think it also reduces the growth of bacteria and fungi.

The trumpeters were just one of the many bird species that I saw in the uplands. I also noted American golden plovers, red-throated loons, snow buntings, long-tailed jaegers, and numerous species of shorebirds. It might seem strange that

Inuvik, one of Canada's most remote towns, is the little bit of civilization

one reaches at the northern end of the Dempster Highway.

multitudes of birds flutter about the tundra, but nearly all of them are summer visitors, migrants from the lower 48, Central America, South America, and even Antarctica. They travel thousands of miles to nest in the far north of Canada and Alaska, partly because the midnight sun provides abundant daylight in which to operate and partly because the summer tundra swarms with insects, one of the main ingredients at the base of the bird food pyramid. (Did I mention that every Dempster Highway traveler needs to bring plenty of bug repellent, maybe even a head net?)

The undisputed champion of migrants is the Arctic tern. Some of these birds travel from pole to pole and back again each year, a round-trip distance of some 22,000 miles. They look like the superb fliers they are: slim, lightweight bodies; long, deeply forked tails; and beautiful, slender wings that unfold into a 30-inch wingspan—on a bird that measures a mere 15 inches from head to tail. I spotted several in the uplands, including some hunting in a small lake. They would hover about 50 feet above the surface, rapidly beating those wondrous wings, and then abruptly dive, knifing into the water. More often than not a tern emerged from such a dive with a small fish clamped in its bill.

The sight reminded me of another time I had watched Arctic terns hunting. A small colony had sprung up along the shore of a glacial lake. I saw one of the hovering terns slice into the water and come up with a four-inch fish. Instead of immediately throwing its head back and gulping the fish, the way a hungry man slurps a raw oyster, the tern flew to the colony and landed on the sand. For a full two minutes it wandered slowly around the sandy shore, seemingly aimless. Was this an addled individual that had forgotten what to do with a fish? Maybe I was witnessing natural selection in action. Eventually the tern reached the margin of the lake, where it dipped the fish into the water several times, apparently cleaning it. I figured the bird was simply fastidious; now it would chug the fish. But no. It returned to its walkabout, heading away from the lake.

After about a minute it reached a nest, which was so well hidden that I didn't see it until the tern was standing on the sand beside it. The tern's mate was sitting on the nest. Tern number 1 offered the fish to tern number 2, which in turn (sorry!) accepted the gift and gobbled it. I assumed this was the honeymoon stage of courtship feeding, a common behavior among terns in which the male of a bonded pair feeds the female prior to an attempt at copulation.

However, after tern number 2 ate the fish, it flew away, and tern number 1 took its place on the nest, which appeared to have eggs in it already. Perplexed, I later asked a naturalist who worked near the lake about this behavior, and she said she had often seen Arctic terns behave this way. They alternate foraging. One will keep diving until it catches a nice fish, at which time it returns to the nest and presents its catch to its mate. Then that bird takes a turn foraging while the other stays on the nest, and so forth. Very contemporary, these terns, with their equal division of labor.

One more vehicle and this would be a traffic jam by Dempster Highway standards. This 456-mile road, all but 11 miles of it gravel, runs through the Canadian wilderness from the west-central Yukon to a point about 50 miles shy of the Arctic Ocean. In winter, an ice road extends the Dempster to that polar sea.

Even after migrating thousands of miles to nest in the tundra,

these Arctic terns still have the energy to hover.

NEAR MILE 65 I STOPPED AT TWO MOOSE LAKE, ONE OF THE FEW DEVELOPED SITES along the Dempster Highway. The development amounted to a small platform at the edge of the lake and several interpretive signs. I stepped onto the platform and immediately saw two moose standing knee-deep in the lake's shallows, munching on pondweed. Two moose at Two Moose Lake. What were the odds? Perhaps the Canadian tourism office had tethered them there. Even from several hundred yards away, these creatures looked huge, especially the bull. In fact, though all full-grown moose are huge, these so-called tundra moose are even huger. They're the largest sub-species on the continent, standing as tall as seven-and-a-half feet at the shoulder and weighing as much as 1,800 pounds.

As I watched the moose plunging their faces into the water to get at submerged plants, some herky-jerky movements in the shadows beneath a lakeside willow caught my eye. I turned my binoculars on the droopy shrubs and watched as half a dozen blackbird-sized whirligigs swam out into the open: red-necked phalaropes. These gorgeous shorebirds were decked out in their russet-tan-black-and-white summer plumage, but it was difficult to appreciate their beauty because they were darting about the surface of the water like lunatics. One moment they'd be zigzagging along, frantically stabbing the water with their bills. The next moment they'd be spinning around and around in one place. I later learned that phalaropes spin to stir up the bottom, dislodging aquatic insects, mollusks, and crustaceans and bringing them to the surface, and thence to the phalaropes' beaks and stomachs.

As I continued through the uplands I saw many more small lakes and ponds—and many more moose and birds, though not every lake could boast two moose or a pack of crazed red-necked phalaropes. People from down south who think of the tundra as a frigid wasteland should visit the Blackstone Uplands. I couldn't swing my binoculars without spotting some creature. Near the northern margin of the uplands, I even saw three caribou—the species known as reindeer in Europe.

Judging by the time of year, these three caribou probably were woodland caribou. A small herd of this uncommon species generally summers in these parts. I say "probably" because, aside from being a bit larger, woodland caribou look just like their much more numerous cousins, the barren-ground caribou. The barren-ground caribou don't show up en masse around the Dempster until fall, though, when they travel from their calving sites on the Arctic coastal plain to their wintering grounds in the shelter of the boreal forest. If you drive the Dempster in October you may want to affix an "I Brake for Caribou" bumper sticker on your car, because for several days during that month some of the 125,000 to 150,000 members of the Porcupine herd—the famous herd that calves in the section of the Arctic National Wildlife Refuge (ANWR) that oil companies covet—flow across this very road.

I DROVE ON INTO THE AFTERNOON AND EVENING, STOPPING NOW AND THEN TO LOOK AT everything from a porcupine to a pingo (a small hill with a core of ice). By now I'd learned some veteran Dempster-driver tricks. For example, I couldn't help but notice the tire-eating shale that sometimes infested the surface of the road. I learned to follow the best pair of tire tracks on the highway, where the sharp rocks had been pounded down by other vehicles, even when the tracks ran down the middle of the road—which they usually did.

I found out the hard way that this trick has a pitfall, though. As I was cruising down the middle of the road, my tires safe from the sharp shale outside the tracks, another vehicle appeared around the bend about a half mile in front of me, heading my way. I swung back onto my side, but when I hit the shale my car started fishtailing wildly on the loose rocks, and I nearly slid off the road. From then on, if I saw another vehicle approaching, I'd brake to a crawl while still in the tracks and then ease over onto my side of the road.

In the end, despite my clever tricks, the shale got me. It happened around 11 p.m., when I was still about 70 miles from my bed for the night. I'd stopped at the Ogilvie Ridge viewpoint to check out the landscape as it glowed golden in the late-night light of the midnight sun. I was the only person there—I hadn't seen any other vehicles for at least an hour—so it was silent except for a whisper of a breeze....

Only that wasn't a breeze I heard. It was air hissing out of my left rear tire.

Right about then I sure was wishing that I had listened to my own advice and brought an extra spare. If I punctured another tire I was in big trouble; it wasn't like I could call up AAA road service. Muttering to myself, I dragged out my lone spare, the jack, and the tire iron, and got to work. I easily removed the hubcap and loosened the lug nuts, but between the feeble little jack and the uneven gravel surface, I was having trouble setting the jack safely. Kneeling by the car, I had been laboring intently for several minutes when a thought suddenly occurred to me.

Bears.

Perhaps you, too, share the memory that flashed into my mind. It comes from a story I've already told. During a previous trek in British Columbia, my companions and I had been diligent about making noise as we hiked so we wouldn't surprise any bears, but we'd neglected to make noise while we were stationary, and a bear on the move had walked right into our midst. Thinking about the plentiful grizzlies that roam the Dempster, I did a jack-in-the-box and scanned the countryside. No bears in sight right now, but salivating grizzlies could emerge any moment from some nearby brush, so I commenced yelling every 30 seconds or so, and about once a minute I popped up for a look-see. And to think that all day I'd been hoping to spot a griz.

No bears interrupted my tire-changing. Soon enough I got back on the road and nursed my precious car tires safely to Eagle Plains, almost exactly the halfway point

This boreal forest landscape is typical of the river valleys of Tombstone Territorial Park. Most of the park lies above tree line, however, and is blanketed by ground-hugging tundra, found here, in its southernmost region, because of elevation and icy Arctic air funneled in by the land's topography.

of the drive up the Dempster Highway. This small oasis offers a gas station, a motel, a campground, a little store, a restaurant, and a bar, though only the bar was open when I arrived, most likely because it was one in the morning. Fortunately, when making my reservation (a necessity in summer) I'd warned the folks at the motel that I might be getting in late, so my key was waiting at the bar.

In the morning a guy at the gas station fixed the punctured tire in about five minutes—I'm guessing he'd done it a few times before—and shortly after eight I was on my way to the end of the Dempster. The second half of the drive isn't as scenic or replete with wildlife as the first half, but it's not exactly nothing to write home about, either. Right out of the gate, for example, the road curved through high-elevation tundra plains that gave me a heady, top-of-the-world sensation. A few miles later I spotted a golden eagle circling high in the sky. And after about 20 minutes I was driving down the middle of an airstrip.

Perhaps I should explain. Periodically the Dempster Highway widens for a half mile or so, creating stretches that do double duty as bush-plane airstrips. Most are for emergencies only, but some get used for less dire purposes. The one I was driving on serves planes carrying goods to Old Crow, a Kutchin Indian settlement about one hundred miles to the northwest. Needless to say, motorists must yield to aircraft.

AT MILE 252 THE DEMPSTER FINALLY MADE IT OFFICIAL. THE ROAD CROSSED latitude 66° 33' N: the Arctic Circle. From here north, the sun never sets at the summer solstice and never rises at the winter solstice, assuming a flat horizon without mountains or the like for the sun to dip behind. I had arrived at mid-morning, so I didn't experience the drama of seeing the sun in the sky at two in the morning (though I'd seen it almost that late the previous night), but the notion of around-the-clock daylight certainly seized my imagination. Indeed, like many people who don't live in the far north, I found it disorienting to have the sun shining during my every waking hour for the week I spent above the circle. Disorienting in a good way, though. I definitely knew I was in a different part of the world.

A pullout with some interpretive signs marks the Arctic Circle. The information is interesting enough, but the life went out of the site when local legend Harry Waldron stopped showing up. A highway department worker with a fascination for the Arctic, Waldron declared himself keeper of the Arctic Circle, and for many years he spent much of his spare time at the pullout. Dressed in a tuxedo and sitting in a rocking chair, he would toast visitors with champagne, recite Robert Service poems, and tell people that they were crossing a milestone that they'd never forget. If I'd had a bottle of champagne with me, I would have made a toast in his honor.

A couple of dozen miles north of the Arctic Circle, the Dempster climbed into the Richardson Mountains. No other vehicles were in sight, and so at one randomly chosen point I stopped the car in the middle of the road, turned off the engine, and contemplated the spare beauty of the wide-open landscape. So simple. The blue of the sky, the blue-black rock of the mountains, the frothy white of water streaming down the slopes, and the green of the tundra at the lower elevations.

And so still. I got out and leaned against the side of the car and for a minute or two I didn't move. Neither did anything else except the streams.

Finally I spotted a long-tailed jaeger flapping low across the tundra, looking for trouble. Jaegers are notorious avian pirates that steal eggs, nab nestlings, or even harass other birds in midair and force them to drop their food, which the jaegers then claim. A bit later I saw a flock of about a dozen feeding whimbrels methodically working their way through the tundra, only their striped heads and long, down-curved bills visible above the vegetation.

What commanded my attention for the longest time was an Arctic ground squirrel. I'd seen hundreds of these cute little rodents scurrying across the road in the course of the drive, but now I surrendered to the meditative mood of this peaceful place, and I really watched that squirrel.

It, however, was not in the same mood. Rushing about to limit exposure to predators—or maybe it was just very hungry—the squirrel zoomed into a stand of seed-bearing grass. Grabbing the base of a grass stem with both paws, the squirrel put its mouth over the bottom of the stem and quickly pulled the plant through its teeth, stripping the seed heads and packing them into its cheeks. Then it bolted to another grass stem and repeated the routine. The squirrel did this over and over for about five minutes until its cheeks had expanded into hairy balloons that stretched from its face to the top of its shoulders. Stuffed to the max, the squirrel finally hightailed it— literally, running with its black-tipped tail thrust stiffly into the air—and headed for its burrow.

Around mile 300, the Dempster began its 30-mile descent to the southern end of the Mackenzie River Delta, dropping 2,300 feet in elevation and changing dramatically in character. The mountains and tundra faded, and I entered a vast bottomland of rivers, creeks, swamps, and forest. I was surprised to see even stunted spruce this far north, but the influence of the mighty Mackenzie accounted for this tree-strewn corridor, which ran all the way to the Arctic Ocean.

I drove along the eastern margin of the delta for a couple of hours and then, at mile 450, the strangest thing happened. I hit pavement. Soon I passed some houses, lodges, and stores. And then, at mile 456, I reached downtown Inuvik, the town of 3,500 souls that constitutes the northern terminus of the Dempster Highway.

I parked the car and I cut the engine and, just like that, the drive was over. I felt a little melancholy about coming to the end of this splendid dead-end road.

But then a heartening realization hit me. It was a dead-end road. That meant I was only half done, and I could turn around and drive the Dempster all over again. ■

Hiking in the rugged, windswept mountains of Tombstone Territorial Park requires proper gear and plenty of experience. Visitors who lack either can find forgiving frontcountry trails near the park entrance, just off the Dempster Highway.

The Far North

The Dempster Highway allows ordinary people

in ordinary cars to venture into

an extraordinary landscape, an Arctic expanse

usually accessible only by bush plane or snowmobile.

You proceed north along hundreds of miles of gravel road,

surrounded by sights and sounds and smells

that you will never encounter down south.

The Dempster Highway starts in the middle of nowhere and goes to the edge of nowhere. You can't get farther from civilization on any other road in North America that is connected, however remotely, to the same highway system that goes to New York City, Miami, and Los Angeles. You'll see familiar scenes, like dancing creeks framed by wildflowers like fireweed, but they're rendered strange by other elements, like the eerie northern lights, page 180, or the seemingly endless tundra.

Taking the Dempster beyond the Arctic Circle is the culmination of this book's exploration of the high latitudes of mainland North America. The journey began in Southeast Alaska and pushed ever northward, ever farther from the familiar and the comfortable, ever deeper into the backcountry, opposite, that sweeps up to the edge of the Arctic Ocean. These fresh and fierce lands of the setting sun serve notice that deliciously untamed places still exist on this planet.

information for travelers

TRAVELING TO THE LANDS OF THE SETTING SUN

For those who want to explore the Far North on their own, here are some sources of information to start you on your way.

Alaska Public Lands Information Centers

www..nps.gov/aplic/
Authorized by the Alaska National Interest Lands Conservation Act, this website and the four centers it represents offer comprehensive visitor information for the state. One of the centers, the Southeast Alaska Discovery Center in Ketchikan, is listed below.

Travel Alaska

www.travelalaska.com
Maps, travel tips, tours and packages, events, weather— all sorts of useful information is collected for Alaska visitors on this website, maintained by the Alaska Travel Industry Association.

CanadaTravel

www.canadatravel.ca
This website orients travelers to all the Canadian provinces and territories. It also tells how to subscribe to *Sojourner*, a travel e-newsletter about events and travel opportunities in Canada.

Chapter One
SOUTHEASTERN ALASKA AND THE INSIDE PASSAGE

Marine Highway System

www.dot.state.ak.us/amhs/
800-642-0066
Eleven vessels provide passenger and vehicle transport to 30 communities in Alaska, plus Bellingham, Washington, and Prince Rupert, British Columbia. Whether you just want to learn more or actually make reservations to travel the Inside Passage by ferry, information is available by Internet or telephone from Alaska's Department of Transportation.

Southeast Alaska Discovery Center

50 Main Street
Ketchikan, AK 99901
www.fs.fed.us/r10/tongass/districts/discoverycenter/
907-228-6220
This Alaska Public Lands Information Center serves as a starting point for exploring these lands and cultures.

Southeast Alaska

www.alaskainfo.org
This website offers information about the South Loop and the North Loop as well as the Inside Passage of southeastern Alaska. Organized by city, including Sitka and Ketchikan, it also gives ideas on traveling off the beaten track.

Tongass National Forest

907-225-3101
www.fs.fed.us/r10/tongass/
Largest national forest in the United States, Tongass encompasses the Inside Passage from Ketchikan to Juneau and includes both marine and mountain trails and vistas.

Ketchikan

www.visit-ketchikan.com
907-225-6166
This friendly online welcome to Ketchikan offers guidance through the gateway and onto the Marine Highway.

Wrangell

www.wrangell.com
907-874-2381
News, events, and visitor information help get you to, through, and around the town of Wrangell.

Sitka

www.sitka.org
907-747-5940
Highlighting the town's blend of Tlingit culture and Russian history, this website gives a taste of Sitka and a form to use to order further information by mail.

Chapter Two
CORDOVA AND THE COPPER RIVER DELTA

Cordova

www.cordovachamber.com
907-424-7260
Complete with live netcam shots of the harbor, plus an online video of the town, Cordova's Chamber of Commerce website gets you about as close to being there as a distant computer can allow.

Cordova Ranger District, Chugach National Forest

3301 C Street, Suite 300
Anchorage, AK 99503-3998
www.fs.fed.us/r10/chugach/cordova/
907-743-9500
General year-round information and updated news from the district of this national forest best known for its salmon fishing.

Chapter Three
THE SOUTHERN KENAI PENINSULA

Kenai Peninsula

www.kenaipeninsula.org
907-262-5229
Homer Spit and Kachemak Bay are just two of the many Kenai Peninsula destinations featured on this website, which includes a thorough map and a downloadable Kenai travel planner.

Homer

www.homeralaska.org
907-235-7740
General visitor information combines with specifics about key events in and around Homer, including annual fests

like the Winter King Salmon Tournament, the Shorebird Festival, and the Winter Carnival.

Katmai National Park & Preserve
P.O. Box 7
#1 King Salmon Mall
King Salmon, AK 99613
www.nps.gov/katm
907-246-3305
www.katmai.national
park.com
Listed here are the National Park Service website and a roundup of other websites chockful of information about the park and preserve and the varieties of ways to enjoy them.

Kachemak Bay State Park
P.O. Box 1247
Soldotna, AK 99669
www.dnr.state.ak.us/parks/
units/kbay/kbay.htm
907-262-5581
Essential information for those who plan to camp, hike, fish, or explore in the state park or the state wilderness park.

Chapter Four
DENALI AND THE ALASKAN INTERIOR

Denali National Park & Preserve
P.O. Box 9
Denali Park, AK 99755-0009
www.nps.gov/dena
907-683-2294
The National Park Service's Denali website offers advice for travelers, a historical narrative of the Denali-McKinley area, and information about camping and educational programs.

Camp Denali & the North Face Lodge
P.O. Box 67
Denali National Park, AK 99755
www.campdenali.com
907-683-2290
Both of these lodging possibilities offer comfort and amenities in the midst of wilderness settings, enhanced by trips into the wild led by knowledgeable and experienced guides.

Fairbanks
www.explorefairbanks.com
800-327-5774; 907-457-3282
Calling Fairbanks a base camp and gateway to the interior of Alaska, the Fairbanks Visitors Bureau provides advice on how to use this northerly hub city as a starting point to explore the inner outback of the 49th state.

Chapter Five
KLUANE NATIONAL PARK AND TATSHENSHINI-ALSEK PROVINCIAL PARK

Kluane National Park & Preserve
P.O. Box 5495
Haines Junction, Yukon
Canada Y0B 1L0
www.pc.gc.ca/pn-np/yt/
kluane
867-634-7250
Learn more about this "gem in the family," as Canada's Parks system calls it. The Kluane website provides background information, specific travel tips, and contact information.

Tatshenshini-Alsek Provincial Park
Smithers, British Columbia
Canada V0J 2N0
http://www.env.gov.bc.ca/
bcparks/explore/parkpgs/
tatshen.html
250-847-7320
Canada's Ministry of Environment offers this helpful guide to the park and its ecology. Here you will find both travel information and important messages about the ethics of visiting the wild.

Glacier Bay National Park & Preserve
P.O. Box 140
Gustavus, AK 99826-0140
www.nps.gov/glba
907-697-2230
Explore the natural and human history of this region online; then use advice you find here to make a trip in person. This park was designated a World Heritage Site in 1992.

Haines Junction
www.hainesjunction
yukon.com
867-634-7100
Calling itself "an intimate community on the edge of a vast landscape," this village invites you to learn before traveling by visiting its website.

Chapter Six
THE DEMPSTER HIGHWAY

Northwest Territories
dmoz.org/regional/north_
america/canada/northwest_
territories/travel_and_tourism
800-661-0788
This directory-type website links to many sources of information about traveling in Canada's Northwest Territories, including visits via the Dempster Highway.

Yukon
www.touryukon.com
800-789-8566
From the town of Whitehorse, capital of the Yukon, this website offers vistas and travel ideas, information and tour offerings covering the entire Yukon, including the 1,500-mile Alaska Highway, traveling up Route 1, edging the Kluane National Park, and ending in Fairbanks.

Yukon Parks
www.environmentyukon.gov.
yk.ca/parks
867-667-5648
From park administration particulars to tips on bear safety, this website, provided by the Yukon government, offers a full range of information to armchair researchers and intrepid travelers alike.

background information

ABOUT THE AUTHOR

Bob Devine has been writing about the environment, natural history, and travel for a couple of decades. Given these interests, it is no surprise that Alaska and western Canada rank high on his list of favorite places. He writes often for *National Geographic Traveler* and has written half a dozen National Geographic books, including *Alien Invasion: America's Battle with Non-Native Plants* and the recently published *National Geographic Traveler: Alaska.* His latest non-travel book is *Bush Versus the Environment.* He lives in Corvallis, Oregon, with his wife, daughter, and faithful dog.

ACKNOWLEDGMENTS

My deepest thanks to Mary, Sarah, and Callie for their unswerving support at home. And a special thanks to Susan Tyler Hitchcock, my trusty editor, for her patience and good humor.

Many thanks as well to Bob Behrends, John Beiler, Buckwheat Donahue, Barbara Fairbanks, Shanon Hamrick, Nicholas Jacobs, Sandy Lorrigan, Davey Lubin, Marty Moe, Carol Rushmore, Echo Sutton, and the great folks at Camp Denali and Hallo Bay.

FURTHER READING

Bob Devine, *National Geographic Guide to America's Outdoors: Western Canada* (National Geographic, 2002)

Bob Devine, *National Geographic Traveler: Alaska* (National Geographic, 2006)

John McPhee, with photographs by Galen Rowell, *Alaska: Images of the Country* (Sierra Club Books, 1997)

John McPhee, *Coming into the Country* (Farrar, Straus & Giroux, 1991)

Adolph Murie, *A Naturalist in Alaska* (1961)

Adolph Murie, *The Wolves of Mount McKinley* (University of Washington Press, 1985)

National Geographic Driving Guide to the Pacific Northwest (National Geographic, 2005)

National Geographic Guide to the National Parks: Alaska (National Geographic, 2005)

index

Boldface indicates illustrations.

Airplanes 15, 22, 59, **74–75**, 94, 114, 139, 177
Alaganik Slough **55**, 61
Alaska
  map 8–9
Alaska Islands and Ocean
    Center, Homer 77
Alaska Marine Highway 15, 186
Alaska Maritime National
    Wildlife Refuge 36
Alaska Peninsula **90–91**, 94
Alaska Public Lands Information
    Centers 186
Alaska Range 114, 122, **127**, **128–129**
Alaskan brown bears 96, 97
Alaskan Hotel Bar, Cordova **48**
Alsek Glacier, Glacier Bay N.P. **150**, 152
Alsek Lake, Glacier Bay N.P. 152
Alsek River 144, **150**
Andrews Creek 25
ANWR *see* Arctic National
    Wildlife Refuge
Arctic Circle 165, 185
  Dempster Highway 177
Arctic ground squirrels 134, 178
Arctic National Wildlife Refuge
    (ANWR) 174
Arctic Ocean 166, 178
Arctic terns 144, 152, 170, **172–173**
Augustine Island 77
Augustine Volcano 77, 94

Backcountry **184–185**
  lodges 92
Backpackers 107, **124**
Bald eagles 18, 36, 49, 58, 59, 61, 64, 144, **146–147**, 152
  immature **44–45**
  nest 25
Barren Islands 94
Bears 18, 26, 61, 151, **164**
  watching 93–94, 96–100
  see also Alaskan brown
    bears; Black bears;
    Grizzly bears; Polar bears
Beavers 144
Beck, Marian 92
Behrends, Bob 50, 61, 64
Berries 40, 43, **134–135**
Bilderback, Dan 58
Birds 144, 152, 167–170, 174
    Canada geese 61
    gyrfalcons 122
    migratory 58

shorebirds **72–73**
    see also Arctic terns;
      Bald eagles; Golden
      eagles; Gulls; Seabirds;
      Trumpeter swans
Black bears 18, 26, 50, 93, 94
Blackstone Uplands, Tombstone
    Territorial Park 167, 174
Boats
  Homer **80–81**
  jet 25
  row **46–47**
  Sitka **27**
  Summertime Sage 54
  tour **16–17**
  water taxis 86
    see also Canoes; Kayaks
Boreal forests 114, **176**
British Columbia
  map 8–9
Brown bears *see* Alaskan brown
    bears
Buses 118
  Polychrome Pass **120–121**
Bush planes 114

Cabin, Denali N.P. **119**
Camp Denali, Denali N.P. 123, 187
Canada geese 61
Canada Travel 186
Canoes 123–125, **127**
Caribou 118, **135**, 145, 174
Cathedral Mountains 118
Center for Alaskan Coastal
    Studies, Homer 78, 79
Chapek, Becky 61
Chief Shakes Hot Springs 26
Chief Shakes Island 23
Childs Glacier 64
China Poot Bay, Kenai Peninsula
    82, 87
Chitina 64
Chugach National Forest 186
Coast Guard 26
Coast Range 13, **38–39**, 144
Combs, Alex 89
Continental Divide 166
Cook Inlet 77, **88**, **90–91**, **101**
Copley, Kevin 97
Copper River 51, **65**
Copper River Delta **46–47**, **52–53**, **55**, 58, 69, 71, 72
  ferries 49
  wetlands **55**, 58
Copper River Delta Shorebird
    Festival, Cordova 58
Copper River Highway 61
Cordova **48**, 49–64, 186

Ice Worm Festival 50
  rain forest **56–57**
Cordova District Fishermen
    United 54
Cordova Ranger District,
    Anchorage 186
Corona, Craig 144
Cottonwood Trail, Kluane N.P.
    140, 158
Crabs **28**, 34, 59, 79
Cruise ships 14, 34
  Sitka 34

Dall's porpoises 29
Dall's sheep 118, 122, **166–167**
Dalton Highway **162–163**, 165
Davidson Glacier, Haines 37
Dawson, Yuk., Canada 165
Daylight
  around-the-clock 177
Decorator crabs 79
Dempster Corner, Klondike and
    Dempster Highways 166
Dempster Highway 5, **162–163**, 165–166, **171**, 174–178, 182
  airplanes 177
  Inuvik **168–169**
Denali National Park and
    Preserve 113, 115, 122, 123, 131, 187
  buses 118
  cabin **119**
  canoes **127**
  Polychrome Pass **120–121**
  sunsets **110–111**
  tundra **124**
  Wonder Lake **128–129**
    see also McKinley, Mount
Dry Bay, Glacier Bay N.P. 144, 152
Dungeness crabs **28**, 34
  otters 59

Eagle Plains **175–177**
Eagles *see* Bald eagles; Golden
    eagles
Earp, Wyatt 23
Earthquakes 61, 64
Edgecumbe, Mount 34
Eelgrass 35
Eskimo potatoes 126
Everest, Mount, China-Nepal 123
Eyak Lake 61

Fairbanks 187
Ferns **40**
Ferries 15

Copper River Delta 49
Ketchikan 18
Sitka 29
Skagway 34
tents on 32–33
Fireweed **130**, 133, **153**
Fishing **80–81**
Kenai Peninsula **108–109**
Petersburg 28
Float planes 15, 59, **74–75**
Foraker, Mount 114
Foxes **134**
Frederick Sound **12**, 29
Fresh Sourdough Express,
Homer 77

Glacier Bay National Park and
Preserve, Gustavus 139, 144,
150, 152, 187
Golden eagles 114, 126, 177
Grand Plateau Glacier, Glacier
Bay N.P. **150**, 152
Grandma's Barber Shop,
Wrangell 23
Grizzly bears 7, 50–51, 64, **70–71**,
90–91, 94, 113, 118, 123,
126, **132–133**, 140, 141, 175
tracks **68**
Trans-Alaska Pipeline 95
Gulf of Alaska 49
Gull Island 2–3, 5, 78–79, **84–85**,
87
Gulls **2–3**, 5, 61, 64, **84–85**
Gyrfalcons 122

Haines Junction, Yuk.,
Canada 187
Haley, Clara 23
Halibut 78, **83**
Halibut Cove 87–89, 92
Hallo Bay, Katmai N.P. 93–94
bears **95**
Harbor seals 58, 59
Hares 115
Healy, Mount 114–115
Helicopter **158–159**
Henry, Don 77–78
Hermit crabs 79
Hlebechuk, Clint 94
Hodges, Ken 61, 64
Homer 77, **80–81**, 87, **101**, 186
halibut 78, **83**
Homer Spit **76**
Hooligan 25
Hot springs 26
Hughes, Mike 94
Humpback whales **12**, 22, 29, 36
Hunter, Mount 114

Ice melt **154–155**
Ice Worm Festival, Cordova 50
Icebergs 7, 43, **62–63**, 64, **66–67**, 152
Igloo Mountains 118
Insects 170
Inside Passage 25, 29, **32–33**
glaciers **37**
Inuvik **168–169**, 178
Ismailof Island 89

Jackson, Sheldon 35
Juneau **24**

Kachemak Bay **88**, **98–99**, 101
float planes **74–75**
glaciers 77
Gull Island **84–85**
Homer Spit **76**
tours 78
Kachemak Bay State Park,
Soldotna 93, 107, 187
Kachemak Bay Wilderness
Lodge **106–107**
Kantishna Roadhouse, Denali
N.P. 119
Kaskawulch Glacier, Kluane N.P.
158–159
Kathleen Lake, Kluane N.P. 140
Katmai National Park and
Preserve, King Salmon
90–91, 93–94, **95**, 96, 97,
187
Kayaks 25, **60**, **62–63**, 86,
98–99
Kelp forests 35, 36
Kenai Lake **102–103**
Kenai Mountains 87
Kenai Peninsula **2–3**, 5, 77, 78, 79,
82, **102–103**, 105, 186
fishing **108–109**
Homer Spit **76**
Kachemak Bay **76**
Kennedy, Terry 59
Ketchikan 14, 15, 186
cruise ships 14
ferries 18
rain 13, **19**
Ketchikan Creek 14
Keyhole, Katmai N.P. 96, 97
Killer whales 23, 49
King's Throne Trail, Kluane
N.P. 140
Klondike Highway 165
Kluane Lake **142–143**
Kluane National Park and
Reserve, Yuk., Canada
136–137, 139, 140, **156**,

157, **158–159**, 187
bald eagles **146–147**
wolves **138**
Kruzof Island 34, 36
Kupreanof Island 26

Leeds, Marguerite 58
Lodges 92
Logan, Mount, Kluane N.P.
136–137, 139, 140
Long Beach 86
Lowell Glacier, Kluane N.P. **156**,
158
Lubin, Davey 36
Ludwig's, Sitka 34

Mackenzie River 165
Mackenzie River Delta 178
Map **8–9**
McKinley, Mount, Denali N.P.
112, 114, 118, 122, **127**
climbing **116–117**
Merrill, Dick 115, 118, 122
Million Dollar Bridge, Cordova
64
Mining **119**
Misty Fiords National
Monument **10–11**, 15,
16–17, 19
Mitkof Island 26
Monita, Darwin 144–151
Moose 25, 59, 114–115, **148–149**,
174
Moose Creek 123
Mosquitoes 82

Nanga Parbat (peak), Pakistan
123
National Estuarine Research
Reserve System, Kenai
Peninsula 78
Nenana River 114
North Face Lodge, Denali N.P.
187
North Fork Pass, Tombstone
Territorial Park 167
Northern lights **180**, 182
Northwest Territories 187
Novatak Glacier, Glacier Bay
N.P. 152

Ogilvie Mountains,
Tombstone Territorial Park
166
Ogilvie Ridge 175

Old Crow 177
Oogruk 35
Orca Bay 49
Orcinus orca see Killer whales
Otters 7, 36, 49, 59, **72**, 87
Oysters 92–93

Pacific Flyway 58
Pendergraft, John 96–97
Peters Glacier 114
Petersburg **28**, 29
Peterson Bay 79, 86, 93
Peterson Bay Lodge 92, 108
Petroglyph Beach, Wrangell 23
Polar bears **164**
Polychrome Pass, Denali N.P.
        120–121, 122
Porpoises 29, 49
Prince William Sound 49, **62–63**
        icebergs **66–67**
        kayaks **60**
Prince William Sound Science
        Center, Cordova 58
Prudhoe Bay 165

Rafts 25, 144, 151, **160–161**
Rain 13, **19**, **56–57**
Rain forests **19**, **56–57**
Ravens 61
Red foxes **134**
Restaurants
        Cordova 50
        Fresh Sourdough Express 77
        Halibut Cove 89
        Homer 77
        Saltry Restaurant 89
        Sitka 34
Reynolds, Brad 58
Richardson Mountains 178
Rock Glacier Trail, Kluane N.P.
        140
Roth, Richard 144–151

St. Elias Mountains, Glacier
        Bay N.P. 152
St. Lazaria Islands 36
Salmon 7, 69
        bears 94
        Copper River 51
        gill-netters 59
        see also Sockeye salmon
Saloons 23
Saltry Restaurant, Halibut Cove 89
Sanctuary River 118
Sargent, Lavena 15, 18
Savage River 118
Scott Glacier 61

Scudero, Jerry 15
Sea chanteys 36
Sea Life Discovery (semisubmersible),
        Sitka **30–31**, 35
Sea lions 25, 49, 58
Sea otters *see* Otters
Sea stars **88**
Seabirds **2–3**, 5, 36, 58–59, 78,
        84–85, 86
        nesting 87
Seals *see* Harbor seals
Seims, Gary and Debbie 92–93
Shakes Glacier 26
Shakes Lake 26
Sheep *see* Dall's sheep
Sheridan Glacier 61
Shorebirds **72–73**
Sigman, Marilyn 78, 79, 82, 86
Silver Lining Seafoods, Cordova 50
Sitka 27, 29, **30–31**, 34, 35, 186
        cruise ships 34
        eelgrass 35
Sitka Sound **30–31**, 34, 36
        wildlife 36
Sixty-Foot Rock, Homer 87
Skagway 34
Slims East, Kluane N.P. 140
Slims River, Kluane N.P. 140
Snow melt **154–155**
Snowshoe hares 115
Sockeye salmon **65**
        Cook Inlet 93
Soho Coho, Ketchikan 14
Southeast Alaska Discovery
        Center, Ketchikan 186
Southeast Aviation, Ketchikan 15
Speed Bump Rock, Halibut Cove
        92
Spruce 59
Starfish 79–82
Steller sea lions 25
Sterling Highway 77
Stikine River 25
Summertime Sage (boat), Cordova
        54, 58
Sunsets **110–111**
Swans *see* Trumpeter swans

Taiga forests 114
Tatshenshini-Alsek Park,
        Smithers, B.C., Canada
        139, 144, 157, 187
        bald eagles **146–147**
        rafts **160–161**
        wolves **138**
Tatshenshini River 144
Teklanika River 118
Tents
        on ferries **32–33**

Tidepools 82, 86, **88**
Tillion, Diana 89
Tlingit 23
Toklat River 122
Tombstone Mountain,
        Tombstone Territorial
        Park 166
Tombstone Territorial Park **4–5**,
        166, 167, 174, **176**, **179**
Tongass Narrows 18
Tongass National Forest 186
Totem poles 7, **20–21**, 23, **104**, 107
Tour boats **16–17**
Trans-Alaska Pipeline **95**
Travel Alaska 186
Troll, Ray 14
Trumpeter swans **55**, 61, 167
Tundra 7, 126, 134, 166, 167, **176**,
        178, **182–183**
        Denali National Park and
        Preserve **124**
Two Moose Lake 174

Valdez 49
Volcanoes *see* Augustine Volcano

Water taxis, Kachemak Bay 87
Waterfalls 18
Weaverling, Kelly 54
Weerstra, Anne 144–151
Wetlands 59
        Copper River Delta **55**, 58
Whales *see* Humpback whales;
        Killer whales
Wildflowers 126, **182**
Williamson, Don 86
Wolves 7, 115, **138**
Wonder Lake, Denali N.P. 122,
        127, **128–129**
Wonder Lake Campground,
        Denali N.P. 122
Wrangell 22, 23, 186
        airplanes 22
Wrangell Island 22
Wrangell King Salmon Derby 23
Wrangell Museum 23
Wrangell Narrows 18, 26
Wrangell–St. Elias National
        Park and Preserve 139

Yancey, Eric 25, 26
Yukon 187
        map 8–9
Yukon River **6**, 166

LANDS OF THE SETTING SUN
Bob Devine

Published by the National Geographic Society
John M. Fahey, Jr., *President and Chief Executive Officer*
Gilbert M. Grosvenor, *Chairman of the Board*
Nina D. Hoffman, *Executive Vice President;*
  President, Books and School Publishing

Prepared by the Book Division
Kevin Mulroy, *Senior Vice President and Publisher*
Kristin Hanneman, *Illustrations Director*
Marianne R. Koszorus, *Design Director*
Barbara Brownell Grogan, *Executive Editor*
Elizabeth Newhouse, *Director of Travel Publishing*
Leah Bendavid-Val, *Director of Photography Publishing*
Carl Mehler, *Director of Maps*

Staff for this Book
Susan Tyler Hitchcock, *Project and Text Editor*
John C. Anderson, *Illustrations Editor*
Teresa Neva Tate, *Associate Illustrations Editor*
Cinda Rose, *Art Director*
Susan Straight, *Researcher*
Margo Browning, *Contributing Editor*
Rebecca Barns, *Contributing Editor*
Thomas L. Gray, *Map Researcher*
Matt Chwastyk and XNR Productions, *Map Production*
Michael Horenstein, *Production Project Manager*
Cynthia and Robert Swanson, *Indexers*
Rebecca Hinds, *Managing Editor*
Gary Colbert, *Production Director*

Manufacturing and Quality Management
Christopher A. Liedel, *Chief Financial Officer*
Phillip L. Schlosser, *Vice President*
John T. Dunn, *Technical Director*
Maryclare Tracy, *Manager*

ISBN-10: 0-7922-5551-8 (regular ed.)
ISBN-13: 978-0-7922-5551-2

ISBN-10: 0-7922-5552-6 (deluxe ed.)
ISBN-13: 978-0-7922-5552-9

Founded in 1888, the National Geographic Society is one of the largest nonprofit scientific and educational organizations in the world. It reaches more than 285 million people worldwide each month through its official journal, NATIONAL GEOGRAPHIC, and its four other magazines; the National Geographic Channel; television documentaries; radio programs; films; books; videos and DVDs; maps; and interactive media. National Geographic has funded more than 8,000 scientific research projects and supports an education program combating geographic illiteracy.

For more information, please call
1-800-NGS LINE (647-5463)
or write to the following address:

National Geographic Society
1145 17th Street N.W.
Washington, D.C. 20036-4688 U.S.A.

Log on to nationalgeographic.com;
AOL Keyword: NatGeo.

For information about special discounts for bulk purchases, please contact National Geographic Books Special Sales:
ngspecsales@ngs.org

Library of Congress Cataloging-in-Publication Data
Devine, Bob, 1951-
  Lands of the setting sun : discovering Alaska and Western Canada / by Bob Devine.
    p. cm.
  ISBN 0-7922-5551-8 (regular)
  1. Alaska--Description and travel. 2. Canada, Western--Description and travel. 3. Devine, Bob, 1951---Travel--Alaska.   4. Devine, Bob, 1951---Travel--Canada, Western.
I. Title.
  F910.5.D48 2006
  917.980452--dc22
                                  2006001874